FIRST-CLASS LEADERSHIP SKILLS FOR WOMEN

FAST-TRACK YOUR CAREER, EASILY NEGOTIATE
ADVANCEMENT, & BUILD CONFIDENCE

LINDSEY BEGUE

CONTENTS

INTRODUCTION

Do you have to be a bad leader to land a leadership position?

Because let's be real—it sure seems that way sometimes. There are *a lot* of bad leaders out there. I'm willing to bet you've met a few yourself at the places where you've worked. Bosses who micromanage—or don't manage at all. Supervisors who seem to take pleasure in adding red tape and bureaucracy. Toxic managers who create stressful, panic attack-inducing work environments and induce employees to quit en masse. CEOs who seem completely checked out of the companies they've been entrusted with.

How do these people get put into leadership positions when there are so many experienced, competent, and empathetic people out there? What vaulted these bad leaders up the corporate ladder while more deserving people were passed over for promotions?

More importantly, what can you do to ensure you're not passed over for opportunities to step into leadership roles, and how can you lead with strength, confidence, and thoughtfulness once you do?

If you've been asking yourself questions like these, congratulations. You're asking the right questions. You've already shown that you're a woman with the desire and drive to lead—and to lead well.

We need women like you. It's women like you who will take the steps to not only boost their own careers, but also grow into excellent leaders who transform workplaces for the better—especially for other women.

Of course, becoming a leader does require hard work and know-how. This know-how is what many otherwise bright and motivated women often don't have, which is what motivated me to write this book. Without know-how, it's easy to feel stuck, afraid or lost. We might feel we've been jammed into a mid-level role without much opportunity to take on more responsibility or leadership. We might struggle with imposter syndrome and question our own fitness to be a leader, sabotaging our own progress. We might fear that the teams we already manage don't respect our leadership skills.

These worries are common and can be overcome. I know this to be true from personal experience. Leading doesn't have to mean leading like a man. You can embrace your feminine side and still earn well-deserved promotions. You can work skillfully and effectively alongside other leaders in the corporate world—both men and women—and enjoy doing so.

Whether you're young or relatively early on in your career and eager to learn how you can advance into leadership roles, or if you're already in a leadership position and ready to find out how to become an excellent leader, this book is for you. This book will show you the exact steps to take to get that promotion and recognition you deserve. Simply being smart and hard-working isn't enough; you need to know what to focus on to enable yourself to move up. Otherwise, you can waste a lot of time and energy on useless efforts keeping you stuck in one place.

With this book, you'll learn what has been holding women back from stepping into high-level leadership and executive-level roles in companies and how you can help change that. You'll get all the brass tacks and helpful instructions you need to figure out what you can do now to earn a promotion quickly, then keep making your way up, earning more responsibility, experience, and opportunity as you go. Most importantly, you'll learn how to become a phenomenal leader that men and women look up to and respect and want to emulate.

Giving women like you the tools they need to become great leaders in the business world is a topic near and dear to my heart because I, too, was once in your shoes. Born and raised in Northeast Ohio, I grew up with a strong Midwestern work ethic. I knew I could work hard, and I had an incredibly strong desire to lead. Yet I, too, struggled with the question many would-be women leaders struggle with: "How do I become a leader in my field as a female?"

Pursuing the answer to this question first led me to pursue a bachelor's in business and organizational leadership. Degree in hand, I then moved to New York City and began a career in staffing and talent acquisition. Since then, I've been blessed to work in talent development and recruitment for top companies like Amazon and LinkedIn for more than seven years. In the process, I have become an expert in coaching others on career development and interviewing.

I now live in South Carolina, where my huge passion for helping women excel in their careers is still as strong as ever. Empowering you to achieve that next promotion truly matters deeply and passionately to me. Why? Because I was once that woman longing for the chance to lead. On my own, it took me a long time to figure things out. I had to learn what I needed to focus on to create effective change in my life. I had to pull back my attention from things that were taking up a lot of effort without yielding a lot of results. The truth is, when we don't know the tools for success, we can end up scrabbling hard for a long time without making progress and run the risk of burning ourselves out without ever reaching our goals.

There's so much I know now that I wish I'd known then. That's why I've written this book to share my knowledge, so you have all the information from the get-go. I want women like you to know what you can do *today* to set yourself up to climb the corporate ladder properly. I want you to make your way up without making the same mistakes I made. I want you to become a great leader—with speed and grace.

We have no time to waste. Ready to move up? Then, let's get started.

1

WHY FEMALE LEADERSHIP IS IMPORTANT

> *"Women need to shift from thinking "I'm not ready to do that" to thinking "I want to do that – and I'll learn by doing it.""*

— SHERYL SANDBERG, COO OF FACEBOOK

When it comes to women and the working world, there are the good statistics and the bad statistics.

Let me start with the good. We women have a wealth of opportunities today that our mothers and grand-mothers never had. Back in the day, young women fought for the simple right to attend college. Today, women make up the majority of college graduates, nearly 60%, to be more specific.[1] In fact, the majority of college graduates in the United States have been women for more than 20 years! Many women are going beyond college to earn advanced degrees, too. An impressive 51.5% of law school graduates are women.[2] And since 2019, the majority of medical students have been women, too.[3]

That's the happy news. Now for the sad news: Unfortunately, women's high levels of educational attainment haven't led to equivalent levels of success in business leadership.

True, we do have some famous female leaders in the world of business. Oprah, Martha Stewart, and Arianna Huffington are business titans who have become household names, too. Yet, if you look at the statistics of business leadership, it's clear that female leaders are more the exception than the norm.

You've probably seen some of these low numbers. Today, women make up only 8.8% of Fortune 500 CEOs.[4] This is an unfortunate state of affairs because our world is in dire need of more female leadership.

WHY IS FEMALE LEADERSHIP IMPORTANT IN OUR WORLD?

Does it really matter whether or not we have female leaders in the business world? Yes, it matters—a lot.

Female leadership is vital. Without it, the business world is a less innovative, less interesting, and less egalitarian place.

I'll prove it to you. Let's look at the two biggest reasons why we need women in leadership roles today.

1. Women need female mentors and role models

Leaders aren't made in a vacuum. To become leaders ourselves, we need existing leaders we can look up to, emulate, and learn from. When it comes to leadership, representation makes a huge difference. We all benefit from seeing people who are like us in leadership roles; seeing them lead shows us concretely that we, too, have the ability and capacity to lead in the future.

When women see other women in leadership roles, they, too, are more likely to become leaders. This is a fact that is of personal importance to me because I was lucky enough to have great female role models in my life as I was coming up. Throughout the earliest stages of my career, I had women I looked up to who were willing to mentor and advise me. Thanks to their support—and seeing these great women lead with strength and passion—I developed the confidence to speak up, take on more responsibilities, and become a leader myself.

Unfortunately, not all young women today are blessed with great female role models. While the business world has changed to be more welcoming to women in the past few generations, gender stereotypes and discrimination are sadly still all too common. In some fields, like science and technology, women are still relatively scarce, and women leaders are even scarcer.

Women in workplaces where most to all leaders are men get the daily, subliminal message that they are not cut out to be leaders, that true leaders don't "look like them." Precisely for this reason, I believe it's vital that more women take leadership roles. We need to do it for ourselves, and we need to do it for the younger generations of women who will come after us.

2. Female leaders bring positive impacts to workplaces

It's a well-known fact: Companies with more female leaders see more positive impacts on workplace policies.

A survey by the Rockefeller Foundation found that nearly three-quarters of Americans believe having more women in leadership positions leads to better workplace policies, such as a decrease in the wage gap and a more diverse workforce.[5]

These are particularly important changes to bring to today's workplace. Making companies more inclusive and egalitarian and compensating all employees fairly are worthy goals that many organizations are actively pursuing today. Women leaders have shown they are particularly keen to and also effective at bringing much-needed changes about.

Clearly, women leaders are successful at catalyzing positive change in the business world and are necessary for mentoring the next generation of women leaders. Which brings us to the next important question: Why are female leaders in such short supply today?

WHY AREN'T THERE MORE WOMEN IN LEADERSHIP ROLES?

Considering the fact that more women than men have been earning college degrees for the last two decades, you'd think we'd see C-suites and company boards full of women at this point. Alas, this is far from the case. Even in 2022, the higher we go up the corporate ladder, the fewer women we're likely to see.

Why, when women, in general, are more highly educated than men, do men still hold the vast majority of leadership roles? Well, the fact is that female leaders and would-be female leaders today face a slew of challenges that often hold them back.

Here are the top five challenges that women face today when pursuing or performing in leadership roles:

1. The workplace sometimes still feels like an old boy's club

Change doesn't come easily, especially if the existing status quo is already very deeply entrenched. When looking at the world of business, we're looking at a world that has been dominated and run by men for, well, centuries. In the past, many businesses were often handed down bloodlines, from father to son, grandfather to grandson. Daughters and granddaughters rarely entered the picture—not in leadership roles anyway.

Today, we have a well-established business culture where men hold most of the powerful positions. Often, when the leaders in these positions pass on the baton, they pass it on to people most like them, usually other men. This is due to a wide variety of reasons: Men often socialize with other men, for example, and thus may feel they know the skills and abilities of other men better than those of women. Men see mostly other men in leadership roles and, therefore, more easily picture future leaders as men, not women.

Basically, because men still hold the vast majority of today's leadership roles, tomorrow's leadership roles also tend to go to men. Certainly, women have always played a vital role in business and economics, but these roles have by and large been more subservient, behind-the-scenes, lower down the food chain type of positions. Yes, things are changing, but right now, they're still changing at a snail's pace, as evidenced by the low percentage of women heading Fortune 500 companies. Tradition and habit act as key challenges in getting women into leadership roles today.

2. Balancing work and family can be difficult

Back in 1989, Arlie Russell Hochschild published *The Second Shift*, documenting a curious phenomenon: Although many additional women had embraced the expansion of their rights and gotten jobs outside the home in the previous several decades, women were still also doing the majority of the work inside the home too —working a "second shift" after they got home from their workplaces.

This situation continues today. It's a well-known fact that the majority of childrearing and housekeeping duties still fall on women.

Why is this so? Well, for one, many families today are headed by single parents, and 80% of those single parents are women.[6] In these families, women are the sole and primary caregivers. Many of these women have jobs outside the home to support their families financially, and once they get home, they need to do a lot of additional work to take care of the children and the house.

Even in so-called traditional families with one male and one female parent, the woman still ends up doing the bulk of the work at home today. Many women report doing the majority of the work needed to care for the kids—whether packing their lunches or chauffeuring them to and from soccer practice, as well as the majority of the household chores or whether shopping for groceries, cleaning, or getting the laundry done.

The work of caring for children and the home is often quite a heavy load. Women with jobs outside the home are thus tasked with balancing those against their family duties—meaning they often need more flexible jobs, allowing them to pick up the kids in an emergency, stay home to care for a sick household member, or work nontraditional hours so they can attend to unpredictable family needs.

Unfortunately, many leadership roles today don't allow for this level of flexibility. Work cultures are changing, but quite often, leadership roles still demand a lot of time and devotion to work. For women who serve as the primary caregivers of their families, it's not always possible to put work first and be available for their jobs at most or all times. This makes women unwilling or unable to pursue more challenging, senior, or demanding positions, as doing so will essentially mean prioritizing their careers over their families.

Consequently, more men have the flexibility and availability to step up to demanding leadership jobs than do women, who often balance their careers with their caretaking and household duties.

3. Women can be seen as "emotional"

When we think of a leader, we often picture someone who is level-headed, reasonable, and skilled at calmly evaluating pros and cons. In short, we imagine someone very rational. Unfortunately, traditional stereotypes label women as less rational and emotional. As a result, women are often assumed to be worse leaders than men.

Why are women seen as emotional? There are many complex biological and societal reasons for this. Women, for example, are known to cry more often than men, a phenomenon that may have some roots in biology. However, girls and women are also expected and sometimes even encouraged to cry—to "let it all out"—while boys and men are often discouraged from crying or expressing their emotions in general—to "man up." Thus, social factors based on gender expectations strongly influence how often a woman or a man "should" cry. Since boys and men are regularly discouraged from showing emotion while women are not, it's unsurprising that women generally express emotions more often than men. Relatedly, women are assumed to be more emotional than men.

Yet, this assumption also carries in situations where both men and women are expressing emotions. In these cases, women's emotions are often interpreted in negative ways and seen as evidence of their irrationality or moodiness, while men's emotions are often given more positive and rational explanations. For example, a woman who expresses disappointment about an error committed in the workplace may be seen as "shrill," "demanding," or "bitchy," while a man who does the same may be more likely to be labeled "attentive to detail" or "having high standards" or even "showing strong leadership skills."

The fact is that women are often judged more harshly in the workplace due to existing gender stereotypes that label them as emotional. This can be a tough hurdle to overcome for would-be women leaders, who obviously can't control all the stereotypes people bring with them to the workplace.

4. The workplace expects less from women

Becoming a leader takes desire, drive, hard work, and persistence. After all, great leaders aren't made in a day. To become an effective leader, you have to devote a lot of time and energy to do your existing job well, so you can take on more responsibilities on top of them and thus move up to a leadership position. You also have to figure out how to manage people effectively, communicate your ideas in motivating ways, and learn from your mistakes.

In short, leadership does not come automatically; you have to work at it. To motivate yourself to work at it, firstly, you need to believe that you *can* indeed become a leader—that as long as you put in the work, you will be rewarded with bigger and better opportunities.

Yet, too often, today's workplaces don't always expect women to become leaders and thus often expect less from women. This stereotype is evident in a number of different ways. Women who are mothers, for example, are expected to work fewer hours or assumed to be capable only of working fewer hours than their male counterparts, without regard to what their true child-rearing responsibilities may be or what they may really want for themselves in terms of work-life balance. Even women who do not have children may be assumed to want children in the future and thus seen as less likely to want a demanding leadership position. In contrast, men are often assumed to want to step into leadership roles and hence often groomed to do so without question.

What the people around us and the environments we are in expect from us strongly affect what we come to expect from ourselves. A man who joins a company after receiving an MBA from Harvard may be immediately assumed to be destined to rise through the ranks quickly and one day help lead the company, even if his starting position is junior. He may be encouraged to join special programs, given ad hoc mentorship opportunities, or simply considered more often for new positions that open up.

Yet, a young woman hired for a similar position may be expected to stay in that junior role for a number of years or even indefinitely, even though she may have equivalent qualifications. She is more likely to have to find out about special programs only by doing her own research, to go out of her way to seek out mentors proactively from a smaller pool of available female leaders, or to simply resign herself to not being the first person coming to mind when the primarily male leaders of a company consider potential candidates for promotion.

Expectations are important and especially those expectations imposed on us in the workplace. Since organizations so often don't expect women to become leaders, fewer women end up becoming leaders.

5. Creating network support can be a challenge

In today's business environment, women generally have a more challenging time than men in finding the support they need. This is because men, having dominated the world of business for so long, have a stronger network of support to draw from.

Men often have established social activities related to work that aren't available to women. Of course, men-only social clubs, the kind that kept women out by rule, are rarer today. Still, many networks today are informally closed or at least unwelcoming to women. Whether it's an informal happy hour to which the male employees neglect to invite the few female coworkers or the company basketball team that's part of an all-male league, women today often find themselves left out of after-work or social activities that could help boost their careers.

This means women have fewer opportunities to meet and socialize with mentors, find out about new opportunities, or build rapport with coworkers, even though these opportunities are invaluable to becoming leaders at work. Personally getting to know the existing leaders of a business, being the first to learn about a new position that's just opened up, or having coworkers in another department rooting for you in your quest to make a lateral move in the company—these are key benefits to network support that many women sorely lack today.

Often, because network support doesn't already exist for women, each woman has to take it upon herself to create her own network of support. Doing this is certainly possible but obviously takes a lot more personal initiative, perseverance, work, and risk of potential rejection. It's not easy, for example, to ask to be included in the team happy hour in which you would be the only woman and to which you don't feel particularly welcome. Whether the answer ends up being yes or no, you may feel you are intruding, don't truly belong, or aren't truly seen as being on equal footing as your male coworkers.

It can also be harder for women to find mentor networks at work simply because fewer female mentors are available. While a male first-year lawyer at a firm may have many male partners from whom he can choose to have as mentors, a female first-year lawyer may be in a firm with only one or even no female partners. The few female leaders at a company also tend to be very busy, as they navigate their own leadership challenges as women and try to provide mentorship and support for the large number of women in more junior positions.

This makes it harder for young women to seek advice, get sponsorship, and gain support. Of course, women can have male mentors, but often, women report feeling more comfortable, getting more encouragement, or being able to receive more targeted and relevant advice from other women. Moreover, because some workplace challenges are specific to women, it is often very valuable for young women to have female leaders to whom they can go for advice and mentorship.

So there you have it: Women leaders are essential. Yet, we don't have a lot of women in leadership roles today because of a number of key factors making it difficult for women to rise up the ranks.

Keep in mind that none of these reasons say anything about women's ability, capacity, or willingness to lead! I know from my work as a career development expert that we have many women in business out there who are willing, able, and ready to step into leadership roles. In the next chapters, we'll look at how women can overcome the obstacles standing in their way and take on the leadership roles they are vitally needed for.

2

COMMON MISTAKES THAT FEMALE LEADERS MAKE

" *"We need to accept that we don't always make the right decisions, that we'll screw up royally sometimes. Understand that failure is not the opposite of success, it's part of success."*

— ARIANNA HUFFINGTON, FOUNDER & CEO
OF THRIVE GLOBAL

We all make mistakes. We're only human, after all, and fallible. So it's important not to beat ourselves up too much when inevitable mistakes happen as we move through our careers. Instead, we need to simply learn from our mistakes, pick ourselves up, and keep moving forward.

That said, we don't have to make every single mistake to learn from them. Thankfully, we can learn a lot from other people's errors, thereby preventing ourselves from making them at all. This is especially true when it comes to mistakes often made in the path of becoming a female leader. There are common pitfalls and errors that new would-be leaders or even experienced already-leaders tend to make. Whether you're trying to land a leadership role or step more fully into your current one, keeping these common mistakes in mind will help you stay on track.

Let's start by talking about the mistakes often made by would-be female leaders: women who are still working toward the goal of reaching a leadership position. There are six common mistakes that otherwise smart, capable women tend to make, mistakes keeping them from being considered for promotions and preventing them from becoming leaders:

Mistake #1: You don't have a clear career roadmap

To reach a destination, you need to, well, have a destination. You also need a map to follow, so you can get from where you are now to where you want to be. This seems like an obvious fact—at least when we're planning something like a road trip, yet one that tends to be forgotten by many women starting out in their careers.

When I ask young women about their career goals, their answers often tend to be very vague. Many say they'd like to "learn a lot," or "grow," or "move up," or even "become a leader." Yet, beyond these nebulous, faraway wishes, they're unable to point to anything concrete.

If you want to be a leader, you must have a clear goal as to what that leadership role looks like. After all, there are many different ways to lead! Do you see yourself as the CEO of a company, overseeing how the entire organization works together? Would you prefer to lead a smaller, more specialized group of people—a team of engineers, maybe? Do you want to innovate and create and disrupt in a creative startup, or do you want to be the calm guiding light at a larger, established company? Do you want to stay long term at the company where you are, getting promoted internally, or do you think you'll need to move to a different organization, whether sooner or later, to accomplish the career goals you've set for yourself?

Make sure you ask yourself these crucial questions even at the beginning of your career. Once you have an answer as to what your career goal is, whether it's becoming the COO of your own beauty empire, a marketing leader at a startup tech company, or a lead engineer at Google, create a timeline for yourself.

Think about the career stepping stones you'll need to move through to reach your ultimate goal and figure out what you'll need to accomplish to reach each of these milestones. Don't forget to plan how long you estimate it'll take to reach each of these stepping stones.

Defining what you want is key. Determining the many smaller steps to get you to that ultimate goal is essential. Yes, it's quite possible that your desires and goals may change as you go through life and your career; however, having a target in mind is always helpful. Make sure that at each stage of life, you have a clear sense of where you'd like to get to, so you're steering your career in the right direction.

Mistake #2: You don't have a mentor in your life

No woman is an island. This adage proves especially true in the business world, where person-to-person relationships matter a lot.

At the start of this chapter, we talked about how we can avoid making mistakes by learning from the mistakes of others. Well, there are no better people whose mistakes you can learn from than the women leaders who have come before you. These women have been through what you're going through now and will go through in the months and years to come. Thanks to their additional years of experience, they have the insider knowledge and know-how about what pitfalls to avoid so you can get where you want to go more smoothly and easily.

Therefore, to become a strong future female leader, you must have a mentor in your specific field or at least a similar field if women leaders are hard to find in your particular area. This is a mentor to whom you can go for support, encouragement, and advice. Most of all, this is a mentor to whom you can go with questions because I can guarantee you many, many questions will come up as you make your way up the corporate ladder.

Many young women I've worked with have told me they're not quite sure how to find a mentor or what to do with a mentor once they actually have found one. However, the mentor-mentee relationship doesn't have to be complicated! Simply identify a woman you look up to who holds a position similar to one you'd like to be in one day and ask if they might be willing to do lunch or have a quick chat. You'll be surprised to find how willing, able, and even delighted most women leaders are to mentor up-and-coming businesswomen in their field!

Your conversations with your mentors don't have to be overthought, either. I have had many meetings with my female managers and leaders, and in quite a few, I have simply asked them, "What have you found to be successful in your career as a woman?" The answers I have gotten back have been invaluable to me in shaping my own career path. These women leaders truly showed me the ropes. They advised me on how to get to that next step I was reaching for and how to quickly get where I wanted to be while avoiding the mistakes they made when they were in my position. Initiate those conversations with the women leaders in your own life, and see what it does for your career aspirations, too.

Mistake #3: You don't speak up or make your presence known

As women, we're often raised to be kind, generous, and humble. Consequently, many of us become reluctant to toot our own horns. Many women go out of their way to do extra work or perform kindness to others at work and in our personal lives, usually without expecting thanks or recognition in return. While this attitude is fine, and perhaps even commendable, when it comes to close relationships or altruistic volunteer work, it is unfortunately not one that will help move you up the corporate ladder.

To get people to notice you as a potential leader, you must first get noticed. This means speaking up so that people notice you. If you've come up with a good idea, be willing to take credit for it. If you go the extra mile, accept the thanks that are rightfully yours.

Too many women doing great work in business tend to "fly under the radar" in their organizations, so their work never gets the recognition it's due. This does not help women advance into leadership roles. Of course, there's no need to obnoxiously call attention to yourself or gratuitously praise yourself at every meeting; however, you shouldn't be shy about letting people know what you're capable of and what you've done for your organization. Don't keep your good work a secret. Make it a habit to share what you've been up to and learn to accept compliments and thanks for your work with grace.

Not sure how to go about letting people know about the great work you've been doing in an assertive yet non-cringey way? I recommend starting with conversations with your managers. These leaders, after all, are people who should be informed about the work you're doing anyway. I personally started scheduling quick one-on-one meetings with my boss, my boss's boss, and other leaders in the organizations I worked for, just to get my name out there. This practice did wonders for my career. Today, I recommend to all young women in business that they work on building these work relationships early on so they can stand out from the very beginning.

Mistake #4: You wait too long to start thinking about a promotion

A promotion doesn't happen overnight. Okay, sure, an official title change generally happens over a single workday, but the work that goes into making that title change happen is usually a months-long or even years-long endeavor.

This is why you need to start thinking about your promotion now if you haven't already. As soon as you get that promotion, you should begin thinking about the next one. Consider each job you hold not as a destination you've reached where you can sit pretty, but rather as a path you've started journeying through leading to the next job up the ladder. Continue on that path diligently until you reach the ultimate career goals you've set for yourself.

Whatever job you have now, think about what you can do to move up to the next leadership position and do what you know you need to do to get there. Can't figure out what the things you need to do are? Take a look at the job description for that next-level opportunity and brainstorm all the ways you can take on more of those responsibilities now. Whether volunteering to lead team meetings or stepping up to manage a new freelancer, you'll find that there are many opportunities for you to raise your value for your organization, as long as you put your effort into doing so.

I also recommend that you start talking about moving onward and upward with your supervisor *today*. Your manager or boss can be your biggest ally and supporter. Let them know what your goals are and where you want to be, whether in one year or five years from now. Then, *ask* them what you need to do to get there. Usually, they'll have great advice for you. Assuming your boss is a supportive one, they'll be more than happy to show you how to take on more responsibility, gain more experience, and show your leadership skills.

Mistake #5: You don't ask questions

The fact is, none of us knows everything and especially not when we're just starting out in our careers. That is why businesses always have mentors, managers, and leaders we can turn to to ask questions and get more information so we can do our jobs well.

Too often, I've found that women early in their careers are afraid to ask necessary questions. They are afraid to admit they don't know something, so they choose to remain ignorant about it. That, unfortunately, creates a much bigger problem. Try to do what you don't know how to do, and very likely, you won't do it the right way. Or if by luck you happen to do it the right way, you're still unlikely to do the job efficiently, easily, or smoothly.

Remember, it is okay to ask questions. If you don't know something, likely it's not something you're already expected to know. Many leaders, in fact, welcome questions. Asking questions benefits not only you but also the people being asked the question, who, in the process of answering, are able to clarify their thoughts, refine their ideas, or even change their minds about a topic due to a new concept your question brought up for them!

The more you ask questions, the more you'll develop the courage to ask questions, even questions that you fear may come across as stupid. I learned this from a senior leader on my team—let's call him Joe—who, during a conversation, told me he'd learned in a humbling way that there are no "dumb" questions. Joe and his wife had gone to a networking event and met an aeronautical engineer, a job title that seemed pretty straightforward to Joe. Joe was understandably embarrassed when his wife asked, "So, what exactly do you do as an aeronautical engineer?" Surprisingly, the engineer himself wasn't flummoxed at all. Instead, he went into describing the many different types of specializations within this field: linear control systems, flight mechanics, wind tunnel testing, spacecraft systems, and much more. In the end, Joe and his wife both got the opportunity to learn that aeronautical engineering has many sub-specializations and that this engineer was more than happy to talk about his own particular specialty.

So do yourself, your boss, and company leaders a favor. Ask questions and use the opportunity to learn and evolve.

Mistake #6: You only do the bare minimum

Today, jobs generally come with very specific descriptions, detailing in pretty specific terms what your expected duties are. If you're a social media associate, for example, your job description may state that you're responsible for updating the company's social media feeds on a regular basis and responding to comments from followers and visitors in a timely manner.

That, however, is really only the bare minimum of what you should be doing if your goal is to become a leader. Instead, what you want to look at is the description of the job that's a step up from yours—whether that's a social media manager, communications lead, senior marketing associate, or something else—and start taking on as many of those duties as you can today. What those duties are will depend on your career goals, but in any position, there will be opportunities to take on more. A social media associate, for example, might step up to manage the social media calendar, coordinate collaborations with social media influencers, add on a new social media platform, or come up with a new social media campaign.

In addition to expanding your role, consider taking on a special project or two related to your job that interests you to show your eagerness to contribute and grow. This way, your promotion to that next role will come almost as a matter of course because you're already thinking big and doing what's required in a leadership role.

Of course, fulfilling the basic responsibilities of your job does come first. You certainly don't want to neglect your day-to-day duties in your quest to take on new ones. What successful leaders do is to accomplish their existing jobs but also go a step above them to take on more.

Avoid those six common mistakes, and you'll set yourself apart as a woman ready to lead. You'll show your readiness to think ahead, contribute, and take charge the way all organization leaders do.

What if you're already in a leadership position, though? If so, first of all, congratulations! Second, you, too, have an opportunity to become an excellent leader—the type of woman leader all people look up to.

To that end, keep in mind the following six mistakes that female leaders often make so that you can avoid these pitfalls in your own work as a leader:

Mistake #1: You're too focused on leading like a man

Women are not men, nor should we strive to be men. Yet, over and over, I've seen female leaders try to change their natural leadership styles to appear more masculine. Some have even trained themselves to change their facial expressions, talk louder, and stand differently to take up more space!

It's understandable, in a way. Leadership roles in companies today are overwhelmingly filled by men, women can easily come to believe that to get and succeed in a leadership role, they must act like men. However, trying to take on a different person's leadership style prevents us from developing our own. I'm a firm believer that everyone has their own leadership style. To be an effective leader, each of us must embrace who we really are. Emulating someone else will only ensure that we come across as unnatural or fake.

Do you find yourself taking on more masculine qualities in your leadership style? Remind yourself that while we've had some great male leaders in business history, we've had some very terrible ones too, and the qualities of these men definitely shouldn't be emulated. Overly-aggressive, overly-risky, overly-demanding behaviors—not to mention harassing, belittling, or abusive behaviors—have all been tied to toxic masculinity. These behaviors do not belong in the workplace.

We've also seen some wonderful female leaders who have brought their own special touch to companies, women who have made their companies more diverse, more collaborative, and more successful. So have confidence in your own innate leadership qualities. Instead of pretending to be someone you're not, let your uniqueness shine through.

Mistake #2: You're too focused on being liked

Bad leaders are rarely well-liked. But not all well-liked leaders are good leaders, either. It may seem counterintuitive, but to be a good leader, you can't care overly much about whether or not people like you as a person or even as a leader. Sometimes, part of your job as a good leader is to make decisions that not everyone likes or that most people actually dislike.

Making unpopular decisions isn't easy, but it can be an especially difficult task for women. Many of us have been conditioned since girlhood to be likable and to people-please, after all! Girls and women are expected to put a high value on getting along well with others, making peace, and fostering collaboration. Those are great qualities, but a leader needs to always balance these qualities with the larger needs of the business or organization.

Say, for example, that you've seen collaborative work take a serious downturn due to your company's switching to remote work during the coronavirus crisis. Now, more than two years since quarantine restrictions first came down, your company is much less creative and innovative than it was pre-COVID. You may know as a leader that what is best for the company is to bring your team members back into the office, at least on a hybrid basis. However, many employees have gotten used to remote work and are quite keen to keep working from home.

In such a case, it's important that you value the company's health and success over your team members' personal preferences. Sure, connecting and getting along with your team is important, but it's even more important to learn how to deliver difficult news that not everyone agrees with or is a fan of.

If you know you're guilty of over-pursuing likability, make it a point to reevaluate your decision-making process. Learn to ask yourself: What is the best decision for the company, regardless of how individual people may feel about the decision? If my choice didn't affect anyone's opinion of me as an individual, what is the best decision I can make? Then, develop your skills to better communicate unpopular decisions in as constructive and nondisruptive a way as possible. Work on getting comfortable with discomfort because being a leader isn't always going to be easy, smooth, or agreeable.

Mistake #3: You don't negotiate

One of the toughest parts of any relationship is negotiation. This goes for your relationships at work, too. Quite often, neither party will be able to get exactly what they want, and a careful negotiation will have to take place to come to an acceptable compromise.

For female leaders, negotiating skills are, well, nonnegotiable. In business, you must simply negotiate, whether creating a solution to a problem, finding a mutually agreeable path forward, or standing up for yourself. Without negotiation, people can butt heads needlessly, companies can get deadlocked, and businesses can come to a standstill or even fail altogether.

If you ever find yourself in a two- or multiway disagreement at work, look for opportunities to negotiate a compromise. Not everyone will be happy, but most will likely be grateful to at least be moving forward, and hopefully, everyone will get some of what they were looking for, even if there are other things they have to let go of.

Because negotiation is such an essential skill for women, we'll look into this in more depth in a later chapter.

Mistake #4: You multitask too much

Have you ever tried to talk on the phone while writing an email? Chances are, either the phone conversation or the email composing went awry, and both ended up taking significantly longer than they would have had you attacked the tasks separately.

The word multitasking is actually a misnomer because, as humans with limited attention spans, we can't effectively multitask at all. When we say we're multitasking, we're usually actually single-tasking but switching between two or more separate tasks in inefficient, counterproductive ways instead of just taking care of one thing and moving on to the next. Trying to do several things at once is a sure way of doing none of them well. This is why some forms of multitasking, such as texting while driving as an example, are considered dangerous and forbidden altogether. You can pay attention to your phone screen or to what's happening on the road but not to both at once.

I used to be a notorious multitasker until I realized that attempting to multitask only left me feeling scatter-brained without allowing me to accomplish more. To be honest, it took me a long time to give up my efforts to multitask, especially at work. Even today, when I'm under deadlines or work pressure, I'm sometimes tempted to tackle more than one task at once. I have learned, through experience, that it is best to put all of my attention on each task separately and calmly cross off one item on my to-do list before moving on to the next.

Multitasking only gives us the illusion of getting things done faster when in reality, it only slows us down and makes mistakes more likely. As leaders, we need to single-task to be effective in our roles and model for others that single-tasking is the most efficient way to get things done.

Mistake #5: You micromanage

In the quest to be good leaders and managers, sometimes leaders end up managing far more than they need to. This is an unfortunate fact because micromanaging usually has at its root good intentions. A micromanaging boss's goal may be to be helpful to the employee they are managing or ensure that work is done correctly. Yet, when we get too involved in the minutiae of tasks that are really the responsibilities of another person on our team, we only create confusion, resentment, and misunderstanding.

At the heart of micromanaging lies a lack of trust. The micromanager just doesn't feel they can fully trust the person responsible for a task to complete it on their own. Thus, they designate themselves as yet another unnecessary cook in the kitchen, "helping" in a way that is helpful to no one at all.

When we micromanage, we create a lot of problems for the people we manage and the organizations we work for, too. People who are micromanaged often feel put upon, watched over, and untrusted. They feel they cannot do their job effectively because every little thing they do needs their micromanager's oversight and approval. In essence, micromanaging ties the hands of the employee. Employees who feel micromanaged are more likely to experience dissatisfaction and a lack of motivation related to their jobs.

I've experienced micromanagement firsthand. In my first role as a new manager, my boss required that we all meet for a daily scrum, also known as a stand-up meeting, every single morning. Yes, it was a sad and onerous daily ritual. One by one, we each had to go through our schedules and explain what we planned to work on that day. This manager was the definition of a micromanager. As you can imagine, she did not allow me to manage my own team how I best saw fit. Let's just say that my team and I did not stay long at this company. Micromanagement is a well-known destroyer of a good company culture because distrust and resentment run rampant where micromanagers work. A bad company culture means employee disengagement, higher turnover rates, and increased sick time and personal leave.

Are you guilty of micromanaging? If so, know first of all that you're certainly not the first person to have made this mistake and that you can change your ways. Micromanaging can be a challenging habit to break, but it is very much doable. You simply need to train yourself to delegate tasks and trust that your team members will complete them without constant follow-up.

Once you let go of micromanaging, you'll see that it improves the work lives of the people you manage and your own life too! This is because when we micromanage others, we essentially shoot ourselves in the foot by creating unnecessary extra work for ourselves! When we poke our noses into other people's work instead of keeping the focus on our own, we scatter our time, attention, and energy, leaving us less capable of doing our own jobs to the best of our abilities. Once we bring back our attention to ourselves and our jobs, we find we're much more effective employees and leaders.

Mistake #6: You don't follow up

While micromanaging should be avoided, following up should not be. As a leader, it is your job to make sure that projects and tasks are proceeding as they should be. This means working with your team members and likely with cross-functional teams also to keep abreast of the status of projects you're responsible for.

This might seem like a no-brainer, but often is not done effectively. Many leaders too often expect projects to run smoothly, even when business experience shows us that it's not uncommon for projects to hit unexpected roadblocks or delays.

Some leaders have difficulty figuring out the difference between micromanaging and following up, but the two are actually quite different. Micromanaging means demanding to know the nitty-gritty details of how another spends their time or the small decisions they make to complete their work. On the other hand, following up simply requires another person to let you know the status of a project, not the exact time and manner they are going about completing the project. Following up is an important part of every leader's job description; micromanaging is not.

Do you know the status of the projects you're responsible for? If not, make it a priority to find out. Check in with the people you manage and work with to ensure that work is on track. Then, work on putting a process in place so that following up becomes a routine part of the business cycle in the future.

If you've read this far, you've likely found yourself guilty of making one or more of the aforementioned mistakes. Don't let that make you feel sad, ashamed, or regretful! That is not the goal here. Rather, if you've made the above mistakes in the past, please take the time now to fully forgive yourself. After all, the reason I'm going over these mistakes is because they are very common ones that many great leaders before you have also made! I, too, have made some of these mistakes, which is why I'm sharing my experiences with you to help you stop making them. What is important is not what we've done in the past but what we'll do in the future. What matters most is not what roles we've filled in previous years but rather what type of leaders we will be in the years to come.

Now that you know what pitfalls to avoid as a leader, let's talk about how to step fully into our leadership roles with confidence.

3

BUILDING CONFIDENCE AND DESTROYING IMPOSTER SYNDROME

> *"A good leader inspires people to have confidence in the leader, a great leader inspires people to have confidence in themselves."*
>
> — ELEANOR ROOSEVELT

To reach your goals, you need to take the steps necessary to achieve them. Put this way, reaching your goals sounds easy as pie. Simply take the necessary steps, checking them off one by one, and you'll get there! In real life, however, many people fail to reach the goals they set for themselves. Why? Simply put, they lack the confidence necessary to fully pursue their goals.

This is why confidence is so important. Confidence motivates us to go after our goals because it convinces us that we are capable and worthy of success. Confidence gives us the emotional and mental strength to truly pursue what we want in life. Thus, as female leaders, we must learn to build our confidence in the workplace.

For many women, however, confidence doesn't come naturally, especially at the start of their careers. A study by Zenger/Folkman, a leadership development consultancy, found that although women score higher than men when it comes to most leadership skills, women under 25 showed much lower levels of confidence than men the same age.[1] "It's highly probable that those women are far more competent than they think they are, while the male leaders are overconfident and assuming they are more competent than they are," the authors concluded. In short, women have been known to "undersell" their experience and accomplishments, while men often oversell their experience.

Why do so many young women doubt their own abilities? Why do women struggle with building confidence in themselves? One of the big reasons for this has to do with imposter syndrome.

WHAT IS IMPOSTER SYNDROME?

Simply defined, imposter syndrome is self-doubt regarding one's skills and abilities. A woman with imposter syndrome at work is likely to feel she isn't actually fully qualified for the job she has and the responsibilities she holds despite evidence showing she is indeed capable and worthy of her position. Often, a woman with imposter syndrome will report feeling like a fraud who has attained her job due to luck or accident. As a result, she may feel a lot of unnecessary daily anxiety or fear, worried that her lack of skills or qualifications will be "discovered" by the higher-ups.

Men can experience imposter syndrome too, but the phenomenon is much more common among women. There are many complex reasons why so many more women struggle with imposter syndrome than men, ranging from the history of male leadership and dominance in the business world to the still-present sexism in today's work environments. Yet, while imposter syndrome is common and understandable, we as women need to work to overcome it because it's one of the core issues that hold us back from leadership positions. We need to learn to coach our inner critics.

Building confidence and fighting imposter syndrome go hand in hand. As we build our inner confidence and come to trust that the experience and skills we bring to the workplace are valuable, important, and worthy of recognition and respect, we will simultaneously see imposter syndrome fade. That doesn't mean we'll never have moments of doubt or times when we second-guess ourselves. Even in those moments when imposter syndrome rears its ugly head, we'll have the confidence to calm down those negative thoughts and take positive action instead.

Clearly, building confidence is a great first step to furthering your career and receiving that promotion. So, how do we go about destroying imposter syndrome? What are the best ways to build healthy confidence in ourselves?

TIPS FOR BUILDING CONFIDENCE

The good news about confidence is that it isn't an innate quality that can't be changed. Rather, confidence can be developed! In fact, many leaders people look up to today often talk about when they were younger and less confident. These leaders figured out how to change that mindset to become the inspiring people they are today.

Learn and practice confidence-building skills, and you're sure to see your own confidence levels rise. In the process, you'll become more aware of your own skills and abilities, more conscious of your inner dialogue, and more able to contribute your whole self in the workplace.

Here are the top five steps to take to build confidence in yourself as a female leader. These tips will guide you in your quest to acquire confidence so that in the future, it will feel natural to trust in your own strengths.

1. Join networking groups

You don't have to build your confidence solo. Confidence-building can be a group effort and might be more fun if you embrace company! Consider joining a networking group that relates to your work and career interests. You might, for example, join an association specific to your occupation, a larger business networking event in your community, or a women's resource group if your company offers one.

By surrounding ourselves with other people, especially women who have similar goals and ambitions in mind or are already in leadership positions, we can take a leap toward building our confidence in the workplace. Every time you meet with your networking group, you'll see women like you doing great work and moving up the ranks of their organizations. By seeing their successes, you'll be better equipped to easily visualize your own. After all, sometimes women develop imposter syndrome simply because they see few (or no) women doing the things they want to accomplish in business. If you change your environment to include more successful women in leadership positions, you'll be able to more easily disabuse yourself of the notion that you're a fraud, imposter, or otherwise unfit to pursue your workplace goals.

Meeting other women with similar goals will also allow you to share ideas and advice. Women who are higher up the ladder in your field can give tips on how best to spend your time and what aspects of work to focus on to derive the most satisfaction from your work and step into a leadership position more quickly.

2. Create a kudos file

In the age of iPhones and Instagram, we all tend to take a lot of photos. Pictures, after all, help us preserve memories so that we can remember the good times and reexperience the pleasure of happy memories. Our photo albums or, more likely, the photos application on our phones keep an easy-to-revisit record of our fondest times for us.

I'm of the opinion that we also need to keep updated records highlighting our work accomplishments. In the same way that we scroll through photos of our last vacation, we need a way to revisit the best times of our careers, the times when we got that hard-to-get job or promotion, completed a difficult project, or led an innovative effort that helped the business improve.

Enter the kudos file.

The idea of the kudos file is simple: It's a repository of all the accomplishments you've achieved throughout your career. The file can be digital or physical but should contain everything you're proud of, workwise. The offer letter for your first job? Pop it in the kudos file. The glowing annual review from your boss? Add that to the file too. A special thank you card from a client satisfied with the service you provided? Don't forget to include it in the file.

I also recommend having a literal document in which you can write down some of your awesome accomplishments at work. Stepped up for a new project everyone else was too scared to take on? Write that down. Came up with a great idea at a team meeting that influenced your company's latest product? Jot down what that idea was. Took on a mentee at work to advise them on their own career? Take note!

I believe it's important to remind ourselves of the times we've done our jobs well. Why? Well, work isn't always easy. We can have bad days at our jobs: projects that go awry, conflicts with our coworkers, or promotions that go to someone else. In those more difficult moments, it can be very easy to forget all the things we've accomplished successfully and get consumed by the things that didn't go our way. It can be easy to lose our confidence. However, if you have a kudos file, you can simply open that up and remind yourself of the many things you're great at, the many people whose lives you've touched, and the many ways you've helped the organizations you worked for succeed.

Don't confuse the kudos file with a resume. The two serve very, very different needs. While a resume serves to highlight what your skills and experiences are for an outside audience, a kudos file is for you and you alone. Thus, you can be creative and unique about what you choose to include! Want to throw in the cake candle from the surprise party your office mates threw for you? Go for it! Every item that shows that you contributed as a member of your organization, whether socially or professionally, is worthy of keeping.

Kudos files are likely more popular than you imagine. I know quite a few female leaders who've been updating theirs for decades, though they refer to it by a variety of different names: the "Ta-da" list, the work Pinterest board, the accomplishment box, or even just "that document where I write down stuff I'm proud of." Once, a colleague told me about her own document, which she keeps readily available and makes updates to regularly. Any time she starts a new position at work, takes on a new project, comes up with a new idea, or steps in to mentor a new team member, she adds a line to this document. The accomplishment, she told me, doesn't have to be particularly big. In fact, some may be considered quite minor by resume standards, but they mean a lot to her by her own set of values.

While the primary purpose of the kudos file is to help build your own internal confidence, it can also have practical uses in the work setting. The colleague I mentioned earlier said she pulled her document out whenever it was time for a work promotion. The document gave her all the reasons that made her qualified for the new opportunity at hand. The information was already right there, ready for her to make her case! All she then had to do to get the promotion was present the information and discuss her accomplishments with the decision-maker.

Having a kudos file can also make it easier to write up self-reviews, strengthen your position in salary negotiations, talk with your manager about taking on more leadership responsibilities, and more. So if you don't have a kudos file yet, create one now. Create a recurring note on your calendar reminding you to update it regularly—at least on a quarterly basis—so you don't forget to give yourself credit for the great work you're doing.

3. Become an expert

Chances are, you're already pretty good at some things and know what those things are. You might be a copywriter really great at coming up with taglines, a graphic designer awesome at putting together graphs, or a sales associate with impeccable phone manners. If you're good at something, you've likely been complimented or rewarded for it in the past, leading to a tendency to spend more and more time doing it, thereby getting even better at it in a virtuous positive cycle.

Chances are, you probably also have things you struggle with, at least a little, or maybe even quite a bit. Perhaps your taglines are great, but your storytelling skills are a bit rusty. Your graphs are easy on the eyes, but your illustrations are less so. Your phone manners are perfect, but your follow-up emails are not that eye-catching or interesting.

My challenge to you is to step out of your comfort zone to become an expert in an area you struggle in.

I know, I know. This sounds scary, but I know from personal experience that going deep into the very things that scare you can be a life-changing experience —for the better, to be clear. Wondering what it was I struggled with? Well, I had a bit of a phobia common to many people: I feared public speaking. In fact, I was so afraid of talking in front of a crowd that I would tremble and have to take breaks when giving presentations in middle and high school. This is to say that, long before I entered the working world, I knew this area was a weakness of mine, a weakness I wanted to conquer.

So I decided to tackle it once and for all. As soon as I got to college for my undergraduate studies, I not only enrolled in a general public speaking class but also took two more advanced level public speaking courses, to boot. I didn't stop there! I added on a course on influencing, negotiating, and argumentation, a class often taken by law students.

Taking these courses truly changed my relationship to public speaking. I can't say that I've banished all fear of public speaking for good, but I can confidently say that I have a lot less fear than I used to. It's at the level where it's pretty easily manageable because I've practiced over and over again how to speak publicly and know that I've gotten quite a bit better at it.

I had to get better at public speaking because I knew I wanted to be a leader, and the kind of leader I wanted to be required public speaking. If you struggle with this issue also, I highly recommend looking for a local Toastmasters club. This nonprofit organization promotes public speaking, leadership, and communication and has chapters worldwide. It's a fun, supportive, and social way of tackling your fears and making connections while you're at it.

Imagine a new you who is good or even excellent at the very things you are afraid of doing right now. Don't you think you'd have a lot less anxiety and fear and a lot more self-confidence? All you have to do to make this a reality is to lean into the things you're afraid of instead of avoiding them!

In the same way you're getting better at the things you already do well by continuing to do them, you're not getting better (or possibly getting worse) at the things you don't yet do well by continuing not to do them. Practice and expertise go hand in hand. Work on a task a lot, and chances are, you'll improve at it. Avoid said task, and, well, you'll get better only at avoiding said task.

Experiment and grow by challenging yourself to get good at what you're bad at now. You might be surprised at how quickly your skills improve and how quickly your feelings about that task start to change! As you improve, the positive reinforcement will kick in. You'll see yourself getting a bit better, allowing the fear to fade a bit and the confidence to grow a little. That will encourage you to get even better and better, perhaps until you reach an expert level in the very thing you once thought you were terrible at. If you're feeling ambitious, you can even tackle multiple areas you think you're not so great at! Change your relationship to those things you perceive as being difficult, and see your confidence continue to grow.

4. Connect with yourself

What makes you unique? What are your passions? What motivates you?

Are you able to answer these questions with relative ease? If not, I suggest giving them some serious thought today. No one can know you better than you know yourself, and yet, too often, we don't spend enough time figuring out what makes us tick. That makes it difficult for us to project to the world the best version of ourselves and tough for anyone else to figure out who we really are.

I think part of the reason many women lack confidence is because they haven't truly gotten to know themselves. There are so many influences around us—from Hollywood to social media to big business magazines—that we're often tempted to look outside ourselves in an attempt to figure out who we should be instead of looking inward to know who we really are.

Don't fall into the trap of believing that you are not as valuable as others around you or that you don't have as much to offer. Instead, learn to value yourself, your thoughts, your ideas, and your contributions. Stop to consider the many facets that make up your history and personality, those unique experiences that only you have and only you can share. Write them down if you'd like to make your self-discovery more concrete for yourself. Where did you grow up, and with whom? What hobbies have you had or continue to practice today? Are there sports you love or follow? Have you traveled to or lived in different places that have molded how you see the world? Are there artistic works, types of music, literary pieces, or other cultural influences that factor into your personality? How do you spend your time? Who and what do you value?

Answer these questions for yourself, and you'll discover that you're a complex and interesting human being with a singular vision of the world, if you didn't realize it already. Whatever that vision is, know it will be an asset to the people around you and the work environment you contribute to. If you grew up with a single mom, you might have valuable insights on how to tap into that audience from a sales perspective. If you know all the latest pop songs, you might be able to find creative, musical ways to connect the brand you work for to a younger audience. The very things you dismiss as irrelevant to your work life may end up being huge assets that you bring to your job and your career.

So make the effort to clearly define what makes you. Remember, you don't need to be, and in fact, shouldn't be like anyone else. Sure, there are mentors and aspirational figures we can look up to, but you don't need to fit into any single mold. After all, you have much to offer the world the way you are. Your one-of-a-kind perspective and way of seeing the world might seem old hat to you but may be inspirational or groundbreaking for others in your peer group or workplace.

5. Focus on building confident behaviors

You've probably heard the phrase "fake it until you make it." Well, it turns out that this advice is quite effective when it comes to confidence-building. Whether or not you feel confident now, if you practice confident behaviors, you will, over time, become more confident.

So what are confident behaviors? These are behaviors that put yourself and your ideas out into the world. Greeting people in a friendly manner, sharing your constructive thoughts with your manager, and giving input in meetings are all great examples of confident behaviors you can implement at work.

Not sure how to get started? I recommend that you begin by going after the easy, low-hanging fruit. What are some ways to assert yourself that still feel like you yet push you a little bit out of your comfort zone? If you're someone who is camera shy at Zoom meetings, for example, your first step might be switching on the video during video meetings. If you tend to arrive at events late because that pre-meeting small talk feels a tad awkward, you might consider purposely coming a few minutes early to the meeting with the friendliest people at work with the goal of exchanging friendly hellos. If you rarely join Slack discussions, you might take the opportunity to contribute an idea to the latest topic. You can make many small, gradual changes to get to know the people you work with better and get your voice out there a bit more. Over time, these efforts will help build trust, both within yourself and with your team members, so that you feel more confident sharing your thoughts and perspectives on a regular basis.

One specific skill you can work on is taking on a more assertive and confident tone and posture. Standing up straight, smiling, and speaking clearly and audibly are all confident actions you can take with relative ease. Many women also tend to use unnecessarily apologetic, uncertain, or self-deprecating language. For example, they may say sorry for things that aren't their fault, phrase statements as questions, or verbally devalue the importance of their ideas. Do you have a tendency to do any of the above? If so, pay attention to your speech, catch yourself, and make it a habit to change the way you share your thoughts. Stop foregrounding your ideas with phrases like "I'm not sure if this is even a good idea but . . ." or "I don't even know if this makes sense but . . ." and instead, simply go into clearly stating what you have to say without these qualifiers.

Building confidence does take time, so don't get discouraged if you find yourself slipping into old habits once in a while. Simply work on continuing to practice them and set new goals and challenges for assertiveness as you gain more experience. As you continue your practices, you'll find some of the confident behaviors you started out by faking have now become second nature and an integral part of who you are.

Now, try these five tips yourself. You'll find that some of them come to you more naturally than others. Expect that and embrace it. Each of us is different, so it makes sense that you'll gravitate more toward the practices that best fit your personality and style. Over time, you'll simply become a more confident person, yet with all the unique quirks and eccentricities that make you. You'll still be yourself but more willing to share who you are and what you know with the people around you.

4

SETTING YOURSELF UP FOR SUCCESS

"An important attribute of success is to be yourself. Never hide what makes you, you."

— INDRA NOOYI, CEO OF PEPSICO

Success doesn't just appear out of thin air. To achieve success, you have to work for it—diligently, continuously, assiduously. You also have to spend your time and energy doing the work that's relevant that's impactful. Otherwise, you can find yourself having put forward a lot of effort only to end up in the same place you started!

Now that you know what pitfalls to avoid and how to build your confidence, you're ready to take concrete steps toward a leadership role in the corporate world.

Doing the right work and doing it well so you can attain success: That's the topic of this chapter. We will go over what successful women have done in the workplace to launch their careers in the corporate world. This will be a step-by-step, how-to guide on what you can do *today* to better align yourself for a promotion and leadership role.

It's time to focus on what you can do now to show that you are ready to move up the ladder. Here are eight important things to start doing now to set yourself up for success:

1. Set up regular meetings with your boss

If you don't already have weekly or bi-weekly appointments scheduled to meet with your manager or boss, put them on your calendar now. These meetings are an essential part of making your way up the corporate ladder. Why? By meeting with your boss, you create opportunities to both inform the higher-ups about what you're doing well and find out what you can do better. It's a chance to discuss how you're performing and get direct feedback on your work.

To be clear, these meetings should be one-on-one, just between you and your manager. The first time you ask your manager for feedback can be nerve-wracking but rest assured that the practice will get easier over time as it becomes a habit and a normal part of your regular discussions. Don't be afraid to be direct! It's okay to be blunt and ask for honest, constructive feedback. It is, after all, part of your manager's job to manage you, which includes giving you regular evaluations of your performance.

Personally, I love receiving feedback. This goes even for those times when I hear things I didn't necessarily want to hear about how I could have handled a client or project differently, about how I could have better managed my time, or about how I might have changed priorities more quickly. Constructive criticism can be tough to take in, especially at the moment we're receiving it. However, it's through constructive criticism that we actually get better at what we do—as long as we acknowledge them in a positive manner and apply them in a useful way. I value knowing what I could be doing better because it allows me to focus on what I can improve upon. If I hadn't asked for the feedback or been open to receiving it, I wouldn't have made all the progress I have made in my career.

Regular meetings with your boss also provide a second benefit: They give you a natural opportunity to discuss with your manager where you want to be in your next role. What is the next step up that you see for yourself?

Do you see yourself doing something similar but in a broader capacity? Or do you want a chance to manage others, to be a mentor and leader of a team? Do you think you might actually prefer a slightly (or even completely) different function than the one you have now? These are important questions and ideas to discuss with your boss. If you don't speak up and tell your manager you'd like to be considered for a promotion or move up into the next level role or make a lateral move, they won't know and won't be able to support or help you to reach your goals. So get them in on your plan.

Ask your manager what needs to be done to get to the point you want to get to. Try to get as much specificity and concrete guidance as possible. The steps you've taken in previous chapters can serve as tools to guide your discussion. The career goals and timeline you've created for yourself can be invaluable in helping you communicate your expectations and measures of success. Your "kudos file" or whatever relevant parts can also come in handy here to help your manager keep in mind your past accomplishments and your skills and capabilities while advising you on how best to reach your career goals.

2. Speak up in meetings

Remember our discussion about building confident behaviors in the previous chapters? Participating in meetings is one of the most essential confident behaviors to practice in the workplace. By participating, I don't mean attending in silence! I mean speaking up to let your voice be heard and your ideas be shared with the other people in your workplace.

Staying silent will not make you stand out as a leader. It will not, in fact, make you stand out at all. The point of a meeting is to bring a group of people together to brainstorm, share ideas, and get to a better solution than any one person might have been able to come to on their own. This means if you're in a meeting, your input is essential to include in the discussion.

Make it a point to add at least one piece of input or ask at least one question during each meeting. If an idea from another colleague sparks a new idea from you, share it! If a coworker says something you don't completely understand, ask for clarification! The chances are that if you want more clarity or information, other people do too. You'll be helping the group in the meeting as a whole to fully digest each other's ideas without confusion or misunderstanding.

You'll find some meetings easier to speak up in than others. Smaller meetings with team members you already know well will generally be easier for you to contribute to than large ones where you're unfamiliar with most of the attendees. Over time, work on getting to the point where sharing your ideas in any meeting situation is the norm versus the exception.

As I've mentioned before, public speaking was a challenge for me for a long time. Speaking up in meetings was actually something I struggled with a lot. However, I'm happy to report that adding my two cents is no longer such a difficult task for me. Through practice, I grew more comfortable sharing my ideas. In turn, this led to others I worked with wanting to hear more of my ideas and even seeking out my ideas outside of meetings. I want the same to become true for you. So start talking. Make your presence known.

3. Take leadership and communication classes

When it comes to becoming a great leader, there's no set end point or finish line you can get to. You can always improve and hone your leadership skills to get better and better at guiding your teams. Therefore, I strongly recommend investing in yourself and your goals by taking classes that will enable you to become a better leader.

Being in a leadership role requires a lot of specialized knowledge, especially in relation to effective communication. I'm a big believer in continuing education because we can all be learning to become more knowledgeable, deep-thinking adults. Taking leadership and communication classes will teach you, among other things, to communicate with many diverse types of individuals. Let's face it: There are many, many types of people out there, all with different ideas, motivations, desires, and goals. Some of us are visual learners, while others prefer written down instructions. Some of us love group work, while others are more productive in solitude. Some of us want to be leaders, while others actually really prefer to follow.

Since you're reading this book, I know you are a leader. Being a leader also means understanding how to motivate and communicate effectively with people who are unlike you—who may not, for example, be particularly interested in stepping up to take on more, as a matter of course, who don't want bigger roles and responsibilities. How can you best help these people succeed at what they do and achieve the goals that are important to them? A leadership and communication course can help you figure that out.

Investing in courses doesn't mean you have to go back to a university for an MBA, though, of course, that is an option. Many low-investment options exist, and quite a few of these are free! I suggest looking for free classes and resources, both online and in your community. Not sure where to start? Begin by browsing what is available through LinkedIn Learning. I know from experience that courses there can be especially helpful for would-be leaders.

4. Get to know your colleagues

We've already talked about how important it is for you to meet with your boss regularly. Now, let's discuss the other members in your organization. Make sure you're taking the time to learn about them too, as they can be wonderful allies in helping you toward your career goals.

Take the initiative to schedule time for coffee chats or a quick catch-up with members of your team. Even if some members don't work very directly with you, reach out and make the time. It is important to build these relationships, especially when you are starting out in your career or are new to a company. Getting to know more team members will help get your name out there and build rapport with your organization at large. You'll also make more friends, cultivate more allies, and improve the company culture through your actions too.

You don't have to stop with your team, either! Get to know members on other teams as well. The people outside your team that you work with cross-functionally might not be the first people you reach out to, but the people you get to know do not have to be directly related to your specific job function or your team. Who knows, a casual chat with someone in another department could lead to you discovering ways to work with each other that help both teams and the organization too. Make room for such serendipitous happenings by carving out time to get to know the people in your company in general.

5. Take work off of your boss's plate

Becoming a leader means stepping up your responsibilities, and there's no better way to step up than taking on the projects your boss could use your help with. People in leadership positions often tend to have a lot going on, so your offer to help will likely be met with real appreciation and gratitude. It will also give you important new responsibilities, help you develop new skills, and position you as a go-getter who is ready to take on more and step into a bigger role.

Not sure how best to help your boss? Ask! Chances are, they'll be able to think of specific projects you can help them with. If nothing comes to mind for them right at that moment, you'll still have communicated to your boss that you are ready and available. Later, when something does come up, they'll remember your offer and give you the chance to step up to new opportunities. Better yet, if you know about a project or idea your boss is working on, you can specifically ask to help with that effort, especially if it interests you or will help you build important skills for the next step up in your career. A good strategy is to offer to take on projects typically managed by someone in the position you'd like to step into next. This way, you'll be able to hone relevant skills for your future job while simultaneously positioning yourself as the natural best candidate for that job.

Offering help sounds like a natural thing to do, yet you would be surprised how many employees simply don't take this step. Reasons vary as to why so many people don't step up. Some are afraid to ask, others are unsure how to ask, and yet others are simply unexcited about taking on additional responsibilities. Since you are on a path to leadership, taking on more responsibility is an essential part of your goal. Volunteer to lend a hand, and your willingness will really stand out.

6. Mentor and recognize employee successes

You don't have to be in a vice president or C-suite position to practice leadership skills. You can begin honing these skills in the job you currently have by taking on mentorship and training roles in the opportunities already available to you. One easy way to start is by stepping in to help orient or train a new employee. Many companies have both formal and informal mentor or buddy programs that will let you do just this. If such a program exists at your organization, volunteer for it. This is a chance to share your knowledge, show people the ropes, and take on a small yet significant leadership task within your company.

You can also help informally support and mentor colleagues, even if they aren't new to the company. If someone asks you a question that you don't know the answer to, offer to help find the solution. Taking this step will give you a productive way to get to know your own company better while also providing support to a colleague and building important connections. Helping out other colleagues and serving as a motivating force will make you stand out as a leader in your organization. Plus, should you need a helping hand from a colleague one day, you'll have a willing pool of work friends who'll be glad to support you.

After all, coworkers aren't just people we work with. They can be our friends, supporters, and neighbors too. For this reason, another part of being a leader is recognizing when praise is due to those around you. Whatever your role, go out of your way to highlight others' achievements and cheer them on. If a colleague receives a promotion, congratulate them, and let them know how excited you are. If an officemate was recognized for an effort they made, thank them for their hard work and praise their contributions. These small gestures of kudos are not difficult to make and may not seem like much, but I can guarantee that your coworkers will notice your kindness and generosity of spirit.

7. Notice colleagues who have been promoted

While many of the habits and practices that prepare and catapult you into leadership roles are similar across companies and industries, some tips are unique to the unique circumstances you may find yourself in. There may be shortcuts or fast lanes specific to your workplace that can help you tremendously once you get in the know.

This is why I recommend that you take notice of coworkers who receive promotions. Why? People who have been promoted, especially those who have been moved up into the types of roles you'd like to make your way into yourself, often know best how to get to that point because they've achieved it themselves.

Find out who these colleagues are and ask them what steps helped them on their path. You'll find that many will be more than happy to share their advice with you. You might learn about a manager who is especially helpful in providing much-needed mentorship, a new training program that gives people an edge in landing leadership roles, or a cross-functional team that can support a lateral move you'd like to make.

Once you're the person who is promoted, be sure to pay it forward. Make time to advise colleagues who ask for your advice or request that you share your story. Doing so will help build goodwill throughout your organization and further cement your position as a leader and mentor.

8. Turn your camera on

We don't communicate only with our words. Our body language and facial expressions are also very important in telling others what we have to say. For this reason, it's important to make sure that you are literally visible to the people you work with, even if you're working remotely.

Whenever you have a video call, make it a point to turn your camera on. This will ensure you are seen as well as heard. People will be able to put your name to your face and better recall both what you said and how you said it. The meaning of what you're trying to get across will also be clearer to people because they'll be able to see your expressions and gestures, minimizing miscommunication or confusion.

I have frequent online meetings; I know just how tempting it can be to leave the camera off. There are many reasons why it may seem easier to appear as a simple black square online: you don't have to get dressed or groomed for meetings, you don't have to clean your house for a neat background, you don't feel like you're on display on a Zoom wall, you can multitask (but remember what I said about multitasking in the last chapter!) and work on other projects while still officially attending the meeting. Yet, when you stay off camera, you lose an opportunity to connect with the people you're working with.

The fact is, we all prefer talking to people we can see, and your digital face is much preferable to a blank box on a screen. Plus, it will be hard for people to remember you if your face is constantly off camera, making it hard for them to remember you when it comes time for promotion to leadership roles. Turning your camera on during virtual meetings can help put a friendly face to your name and to put your name on the list of leaders.

5

DEFINING YOUR LEADERSHIP STYLE

66 *"I learned to always take on things I'd never done before. Growth and comfort do not coexist."*

— GINNI ROMETTY, EXECUTIVE
CHAIRPERSON OF IBM

E very leader has a leadership style, and this style defines how the leader functions, makes decisions, and troubleshoots problems. Therefore, defining a leadership style early on in your career is essential. Since you are in or preparing to step into a leadership role, knowing what your leadership style is will determine what type of leader you will be.

Each leadership style has its strengths and weaknesses, which makes different styles more appropriate and effective for some functions than others. Some styles create more distance between the leader and the led, while others close that gap. Some are more hands-on and mentorship-oriented, while others are hands-off and individual-oriented. So think carefully about what kind of style the roles you plan to step into will require. You might want to focus on one specific style or find a combination of styles to create a unique amalgam that works for you. Whichever styles you choose, be aware of the pitfalls to avoid so you can take advantage of the strengths without succumbing to the weaknesses.

To give you a sense of the options available to you, here are the seven primary leadership styles we most commonly find in use among leaders today:

1. Autocratic Leadership

An autocratic leader usually leads with a very top-down approach. The military, for example, is an example of an organization that tends to have a more autocratic approach to leadership, where the higher-ranking person's commands must be obeyed by those lower down the totem pole without question.

An autocratic style is also known as a "command and control approach" to leadership. Orders come from the top and are expected to be followed without delay or pushback. Input from team members isn't highly valued; rather, team members are expected to value the opinions of the leader.

One of the benefits of an autocratic style is that it offers a lot of control. If a project or goal really should only be accomplished in one way, an autocratic leadership style can be useful for bringing clear focus and direction to the task at hand. This can help goals get accomplished more efficiently. The time that might otherwise be spent discussing various ideas, parsing opinions, or arguing for one course of action over another gets saved because most team members aren't asked to weigh in. Instead, they are simply informed of what needs to be done. If a team has mostly novice members who would really learn more by following directions than by trying to come up with their own way of doing things, the autocratic leadership style can be useful.

The autocratic style does come with challenges, however. Many employees today highly value the ability to give input and help shape the direction a team takes. When team members aren't given the opportunity to weigh in, they may lose motivation and morale. The autocratic style also relies very heavily on the leader, which can become problematic because no one person can make the best decisions on their own all the time. A leader might end up making subpar decisions due to a lack of broader input, engage in unnecessary micromanagement of tasks, or come across as intimidating due to the being given so much power over the direction of the team.

While an autocratic style works in some organizations, it tends not to be popular in today's workplace. This is because the style doesn't allow for much collaboration and consensus building, features that younger generations especially tend to value. If you decide to choose this leadership approach, make sure it's truly appropriate for the type of position you hold and the organization you are part of.

2. Authoritative Leadership

An authoritative leader guides her team assertively but without being overly controlling. Rather than dictate exactly what must be done, an authoritative leader instead serves as a guiding light for the team, working with its members to develop an appropriate roadmap to follow. This way, other team members have an opportunity to put forward their best ideas and offer their expertise in deciding the best direction to take to accomplish goals.

Many authoritative leaders are called visionary or motivating because these types of leaders often inspire people to follow in their direction. Rather than strong-arming people into doing their bidding, authoritative leaders are able to encourage the people around them to trust in their leadership as a matter of course. People who gravitate toward authoritative leaders are often eager for guidance and feedback in order to do their work better. In short, authoritative leaders guide people to achieve great things, thereby contributing to a greater sense of achievement.

Authoritative leaders are generally quite adaptable because they are adept at providing direction to different types of individuals. Usually, authoritative leaders take the time to get to know each member of a team on an individual level so they can customize the feedback they give to team members. In this sense, authoritative leaders are pretty hands-on. One thing such leaders should be aware of is that authoritative behavior can sometimes go too far into micromanaging behavior. Make sure to provide direction rather than getting too much into the weeds of any team member's individual function.

An authoritative style is known to be reliable, depend-able, and trustworthy. While all members of the team are invited to share their opinions, the authoritative leader is responsible for weighing those opinions carefully and selecting the next steps. This means that the structure of a team with an authoritative leader is not entirely flat; the leader is not on equal footing with all team members because the leader is still very much expected to decide on courses of action and push the team in the direction she deems best. To take on this leadership approach, you must find a balance between making sure all voices are heard and making tough decisions that may not always be popular.

3. Pacesetting Leadership

A pacesetting leader defines success primarily by reaching specific milestones and goals. For this type of leader, how team members go about accomplishing a goal is less important than whether or not they reach the goal successfully within the set time period. For example, if the goal for a business development team is to sign ten new clients in the coming quarter, a pacesetting leader is likely to give her team members a lot of leeway and freedom as to how they go about finding new clients—as long as those ten new clients are signed. Pacesetting leaders are especially common in sales departments, where often, both individuals and the team as a whole are given time-limited sales goals to achieve.

Pacesetting leaders are known for setting high standards and ambitious goals that must be pursued assiduously. The team members may view the leader as ambitious or perfectionistic, often seeking to not only meet but also exceed goals. The vision and energy of pacesetting leaders can be inspiring for the teams they manage. Often, these leaders will be the hardest working member of the team, setting a model for others to follow. These leaders are great at getting the best performance out of high-achieving employees who like being pushed to do their best. Teams with members who already have a lot of experience usually do best with this type of leader. Employees are given the opportunity to work toward urgent push goals by putting their existing knowledge and skills into practice.

Basically, a pacesetting leader sets a high bar and motivates her team members to reach that bar. This style works especially well for energetic entrepreneurs, which is why pacesetting leaders are often seen at startup tech companies. Because startups are generally expected to grow quickly, leaders at these companies have to wear a lot of hats and move fast. That gives leaders little time to get involved in the minutiae of how each team member gets their job done. Instead, leaders need to bring on team members they can trust to get the work completed.

People who like to work independently often prefer pacesetting leaders because this style allows for a lot of freedom. However, those who prefer a more hands-on leader may desire a different type of manager who is more willing to guide them step-by-step. Not all people thrive in high-energy environments, after all. Some employees might find that pacesetting leaders create work environments that feel too highly stressed. If you use this leadership style, make sure the goals you set are ambitious but not impossible. If your team repeatedly isn't able to meet its goals, the team will, over time, lose motivation and drive, potentially leading to employee burnout.

4. Democratic Leadership

Like the authoritative leader, the democratic leader also seeks team members' opinions before making decisions. In the democratic leader's case, however, the general opinions of the people on her team hold a stronger sway in the decision-making process. While an authoritative leader might listen to team members yet make a decision contrary to popular opinion, a democratic leader is more likely to consider the opinions of her team members of equal importance as her own and seek to reflect the majority rule in the decisions they make.

The democratic leadership style is sometimes also called participative leadership because it's a style that encourages all members of the team to participate in the decision-making process. Inclusivity is key for this leadership style. Listening to employees, practicing strong communication skills, and sharing responsibility for both successes and shortcomings are important. Since the power of the collective group is strongly emphasized, the democratic leadership style is great for fostering collaboration among team members. Instead of individuals taking blame or credit, the group as a whole is encouraged to figure out what the problems are and come up with solutions together.

As a very common and popular style, democratic leadership can really be appropriate for any level of an organization. It encourages communication between members, so opinions and ideas are shared with all. One of the challenges of the style, however, is its flat structure. Since everyone's opinion must be considered, decision-making can feel decentralized, sometimes making it tougher for teams to come to a final decision to move forward. This issue can be especially a challenge for distributed teams that may be working from multiple locations, without a lot of face time that brings the group together.

The democratic leadership style can be helpful for making employees feel that their opinion matters and will directly influence decisions that are made. It breeds trust and encourages a sense of empowerment. However, this leadership can be less effective when the course of action that is best for the business is an unpopular one that goes against general approval and agreement. As a result, a key quality of an effective democratic leader is consensus building so that decisions are made more easily without undue roadblocks due to conflicting opinions.

5. Coaching Leadership

The coaching leadership style requires a lot of mentorship of employees on the part of the leader. A coaching leader is one who tends to be more involved and in close, frequent communication, clearly guiding team members not only on what to do but also how to do it. Of course, some coaching leaders can be more involved than others. A more hands-off coaching leader might simply step in to offer mentorship when a team member asks for help or to reorient a project if it has gone off course, while a more hands-on coaching leader might offer guidance and direction at every step of a project. A coaching leader also considers how the team can best work together. By paying attention to the team members' individual gifts, the leader can see how those talents can all fit together to form a cohesive goal.

The sense of individual growth and accomplishment for each team member is of the utmost importance to a coaching leader. If you take on this leadership style, your main leadership actions will be giving members of your team opportunities to grow by providing opportunities to take on new tasks while offering guidance, encouragement, and constructive feedback throughout. You might also encourage a coaching mentality throughout your team, giving other members opportunities to teach or learn new skills from each other.

A coaching leader is appreciated by many employees who care about their individual growth. After all, here's a leader that recognizes the unique contribution of every team member! With a coaching leader, team members can get support while developing their skills and learning to troubleshoot problems. Teams often bring together a wide variety of individuals from diverse backgrounds and points of view, allowing for an exciting exchange of ideas. This often helps to build a strong and positive company culture because people feel like they are growing as individuals, not simply completing a goal for the business. Coaching leaders are often remembered and revered by the people they lead, even after those people leave the company.

Employees who appreciate a lot of clear direction often prefer a coaching leader because this type of leader offers significant guidance and feedback. However, coaching is an intensive skill, so nurturing employees with a coaching leadership style can be taxing on the leader as it requires a high investment of time, patience, and attention. However, employees who prefer to learn or work independently might find even well-meaning coaching leaders somewhat overbearing because of the closer and more frequent contact and check-ins common to this type of leadership style. Consider the unique preferences and needs of your individual team members when deciding whether or not a coaching approach is the appropriate one to take with them.

6. Affiliate Leadership

An affiliate leader is one who is best known for connecting with and inspiring employees through a common vision. Usually considered a veritable people person, an affiliate leader pays close attention to the emotions of the people she manages. She is able to easily read the mood of a meeting or the culture of her team and adapt her tone, speech, and manner accordingly so that people feel they are listened to and reassured.

The affiliate leader is great at fostering collaboration and teamwork. Since she is able to tap into her own emotional intelligence, she can inspire her team members to follow her plan. Often, affiliate leaders are great at communicating their ideas in persuasive ways, getting people excited about achieving business goals.

The affiliate leadership style is especially effective when working with people who enjoy making progress toward a bigger vision. These bigger ideas can be very motivating, especially in those cases when the smaller, immediate tasks that need to be done can feel repetitive or uninspiring on their own. However, a challenge with this style is that the team's focus can get too far away and nebulous. At times, affiliate leaders need to be reminded to focus on more immediate, day-to-day issues over big vision goals.

Since she is attuned to emotions, an affiliate leader especially shines in times of stress when tensions run high. She can quickly sense a team member's sentiments about a situation and connect with them not only on an intellectual level but also an emotional level. The opposite of a cold and calculating leader, an affiliate leader carefully considers not just the objective facts of an issue but also the subjective feelings surrounding it. The way people may feel about a project, problem, or proposed course of action is given serious attention. While an affiliate leader may seem too touchy-feely for some employees, others deeply appreciate the human empathy, warmth, and consideration shown by these leaders.

7. Laissez-Faire Leadership

The laissez-faire leadership style is the most hands-off model of management. This style largely trusts team members to make the right decisions and thus leaves them to do their job without providing a lot of direction, input, or guidance. The motto of a laissez-faire leader may be best described as "let people swim with the current." Instead of actively trying to mold or shape people or projects, laissez-faire leaders are more interested in seeing how people or projects shape up when given free rein.

Sometimes also referred to as a delegative leadership style, the laissez-faire leadership relies strongly on delegation. Tasks or projects are given to team members, who are then more or less left on their own to do their work. This means leaders trust their team members, relying on them to get the job done as practically, efficiently, and productively as possible. Employees aren't bogged down by feedback or guidance and are instead encouraged to make their own decisions, employing their own skills, creativity, and best ideas.

This leadership style is so open and trusting, it works best when managing employees who are already experienced and self-motivated. In short, laissez-faire leaders perform the best when the people they manage are already experts in their fields and know the steps that need to be taken to accomplish goals. In contrast, if many employees are brand new to a role and require training and mentorship—or if they simply perform better with the direct pressures of external motivation —the laissez-faire leadership approach may not be as effective because it relies too heavily on the employee to act on their own. Since the leader doesn't step in to dictate a direction in this style, this type of leadership can also sometimes lead to conflicts among team members who have very different ideas about how a task should be accomplished. At times, the question of who is in fact the leader or ultimately responsible for reaching goals can get difficult to resolve. It's essential to keep these potential pitfalls in mind when taking on this leadership style.

HOW TO CHOOSE THE RIGHT LEADERSHIP STYLE FOR YOU

While some of the above leadership styles are more popular or common than others in today's workplace, they all have their strengths and weaknesses. A style that works well in one company or one function may not work in another. Thus, it's really important to consider which leadership style is the right fit for you, your unique leadership role, and your organization.

When choosing which leadership style works best for you, the first thing to consider is your own personality. Get to know yourself and figure out which style comes more naturally to you. If you've always loved closely mentoring people, the coaching style might be one that you gravitate to. If you're very much a think-on-your-feet and move quickly kind of person, you might thrive as a pacesetting leader. If you automatically put a high value on the opinions of the majority and consensus building, a democratic style might be more to your taste. Likely, you'll find a few styles from the list above capturing aspects of your personality, which will help narrow down your options for leadership styles.

Once you know which styles mesh with your personality, consider the specific needs of your position or organization. If, for example, your company has named empathy as a core value for the organization, you might consider leaning more heavily into your affiliate leadership qualities. On the other hand, if your team members are mostly entry level and need significant training and mentorship, you might emphasize your coaching leadership qualities.

Once you've identified the style or styles that work best for yourself and your situation, it's time to start implementing these new skills. Try out the new leadership styles and practice them hands-on. As you gain more experience as a leader, you might learn you need to incorporate additional leadership styles or switch styles altogether. Give yourself time and space for this learning process.

Since our environments and the people we work with can change quite quickly in the twenty-first-century workplace, it's important to be flexible with your leadership style. Don't assume that just because one leadership style worked well in one situation in the past, it will always be the best one to stick to in the future. A team you managed well with a coaching leadership style when most of the members were just hired might now work better under a laissez-faire leadership style because they have gained enough experience not to need as much hands-on support. As a leader, you need to be agile and willing to change your leadership style depending on the situation you're facing.

6

NEGOTIATING FOR YOURSELF & ELIMINATING FEAR

66 *"Don't bargain yourself down before you get to the table."*

— CAROL FROHLINGER, PRESIDENT OF
NEGOTIATING WOMEN, INC.

As women leaders, we are living in times that can often feel confusing. On the one hand, we are told that the business world is cutthroat, and we have to adapt to its winner-takes-all environment by competing hard to outdo others and succeed. On the other hand, we are told that if we strongly advocate for ourselves, we'll be written off as harsh, selfish, and, well, bitchy women.

Neither of these assertions accurately reflect the reality of the working world today, which can certainly be competitive, but in a much more complex and nuanced way than many people assume. Business—and leadership in business—is not a zero-sum game in which the most antagonistic and blatantly competitive people succeed. Rather, there are a lot of opportunities for kind, empathetic leaders, leaders who treat the people they work with not as competitors they need to outdo but rather as collaborators they can succeed with.

What I encourage you to focus on to succeed as a female leader today is not competition but negotiation. Competition assumes there are winners and losers, while negotiation opens up the possibility for everyone to come out on top by making smart choices and trade-offs along the way. Instead of antagonistically trying to compete your way to the top, I want to help you and other women learn how to negotiate for yourselves in the workplace without changing who you are.

WHY NEGOTIATION MATTERS

Negotiation often gets a bad rap, especially among women. Since so many of us grew up being taught to value sharing, yielding, and supporting others, we sometimes can feel uncomfortable asking for things we ourselves want and deserve. Yet, negotiating isn't a selfish or unnecessarily demanding act. Negotiating is simply advocating to receive our fair due. It's also an essential skill for succeeding in business.

The fact is, becoming a leader as a woman is near impossible if you don't know how to negotiate. As negotiation expert, Dr. Chester L. Karrass has famously said, "In business as in life, you don't get what you deserve, you get what you negotiate." Thus, if a leadership position is what you want in business, you need to learn to negotiate so that you can step into the position and get that title.

Negotiating is, at its core, a collaborative act that seeks to find the best outcome for all parties involved. Since negotiating is collaborative, it doesn't require any harsh or aggressive methods to achieve its ends. This is an especially important point because there are many voices in the world today stating that, for a woman to be an effective leader or advance her career, she must be less soft and empathetic and instead act more competitive and combative. Women are told they need to "toughen up" and "act like a man." Yet, nothing could be further from the truth. A study by the Harvard Business Review found that eight of the ten characteristics people most wanted in their leaders were qualities associated with femininity. Clearly, successful female leaders don't need to change their personalities to appear more like men. Rather, they simply need to learn to negotiate.

What does it mean to negotiate? Negotiating means standing up to assertively advocate for yourself while staying true to your true and honest self. While this important skill is essential for both male and female leaders, it is women who often need more help with developing their negotiation skills. This is due to societal norms that have long discouraged women from learning and practicing effective negotiating skills. Since many of us have been taught since we were little girls that we shouldn't ask for what we want—but rather wait in silence or simply yield to what other people want—we can find the act of negotiating difficult, embarrassing, or challenging.

In fact, many women choose not to stand up and negotiate for themselves, largely due to fear. Would-be women leaders are not negotiating for opportunities because they are afraid of being judged negatively or looked down upon. As a result, women are not only losing out on leadership roles but also fair salaries, benefits, and other perks too! A remarkable 32% of women admitted to not negotiating their salary at the time of hire specifically because they were afraid of being told no or even having the job offer rescinded completely.

Yet, having worked as a recruiter, I can tell you from personal experience that companies often have significantly more flexibility than they admit to when extending their initial job offer. This means the fear that a job offer will be rescinded is just not realistic. Rather, companies are accustomed to salary negotiations and often expect and are open to them. The times when I've engaged in salary negotiations, I've had mostly positive experiences where the company came back with a higher offer than initially given. The worst that can happen through a salary negotiation is that the offer remains unchanged. Even if the request for a higher salary is denied, asking for one leaves you in no worse position than you were in before! There is literally no harm in engaging in negotiation, yet even today, nearly a third of women are too fearful of doing it.

HOW TO TACKLE FEAR OF NEGOTIATING

It's interesting how, even when we know a fear is not realistic, we can still, well, feel a lot of fear! This uncomfortable feeling of fear is why we so often avoid tough conversations that could open us up to better opportunities. In such cases, our fears are best conquered by being seen through a different lens. Rather than avoiding the things that make us afraid, embrace them as fun challenges and find ways to gradually challenge your fears until they dissipate.

Rest assured that I'm not suggesting you immediately rush into your boss's office and demand a raise tomorrow morning. Rather, take things a small step at a time, setting one tiny goal for yourself after another.

1. Do Your Research

One of the best ways to overcome your fears is by gaining knowledge. Having a clear and factual picture of the topic you wish to negotiate about can be incredibly helpful in giving you confidence that the negotiation-related requests you're making are reasonable and desirable.

It helps to back up your negotiating points with facts, so make sure you've got numbers on your side before heading to the negotiating table. For example, before asking for a raise, research what the average salary is for the position you're in. Career and job seeker websites often have this information freely available. By knowing that the new salary you're asking for is in line with what is standard, you'll feel more confident that your request is a logical one with a good chance of being met.

Try to also look into ways that both the person you are negotiating with, and you may benefit. Put yourself in the other party's shoes. If you're negotiating with your boss about moving up to a position with more leadership responsibilities, it would be helpful to know how such a move would benefit your boss. In your research, you might discover there are some time-consuming tasks your boss really dislikes doing, which you would like the opportunity to take on in order to gain managerial experience. Armed with this knowledge, you'll be able to show your boss that giving you a chance at a role with more responsibility can be a win-win for both of you.

Consider the other party's potential counterarguments. Are there things you plan to say they might disagree with or have a different point of view on? Have a sense of what these things might be, then research what an effective response might be. By anticipating the other side's viewpoint, you'll be better able to prepare yourself for whatever comes up during your negotiation discussion.

2. Don't Confront – Collaborate

The attitude you bring to your negotiations matters a lot. If you come to a meeting ready to fight, it's much more likely you'll end up in an antagonistic exchange.

To avoid going this route, think of negotiation not as a one-way argument on your end to achieve your own ends but rather as a two-way discussion to find a solution that makes all parties happier. If you approach negotiation this way, you'll be able to take on a much more collaborative tone. There is no reason to be pushy, aggressive, or argumentative. Rather, you can simply assert yourself directly and advocate not just for yourself but also for the benefits that other parties will gain.

To this end, I recommend bringing your whole self to negotiations. You don't have to be entirely cold and businesslike even when taking on business-related negotiations! Rather, connecting on a human level is a highly valuable tactic. Do the things that make people comfortable and more likely to relate to each other in a personal way, whether that's by making small talk at the beginning of the negotiation meeting so you can get to know each other better or sharing why the issue you're negotiating for is beneficial on a personal level for your long-term career goals.

Envision yourself as a problem solver that is focused on bringing success to everyone. Keep in mind not just what you want out of the negotiation but what everyone else does too, and then look for solutions that best meet all of those various wants. Be willing to listen so you can have a very good sense of what is at stake for the others in this negotiation discussion. Then, be creative and flexible when looking for solutions. The end agreement you reach may be somewhat different from the initial ideas you went in with; be open to edits and changes to your vision, as long as you're able to negotiate for the aspects that are most important to you.

3. Start small

Great negotiating takes practice. It is, after all, a skill you can learn and get better at. Rather than make your first attempt at negotiation a super stressful, high-stakes discussion about the future of your career, start learning to negotiate by beginning with relatively low-stakes interactions. This will help you build both confidence and skills so that, later on, you can more readily take on those tougher negotiating situations.

Often, women who have trouble negotiating have difficulty initiating conversations in general. If this is the case for you, a good first goal would be to start a basic conversation this week with someone you don't know well. This can be a stranger at the bus stop, a check-out clerk at the supermarket, or, if you'd like to limit your efforts to the work setting, a person at your office you don't normally stop to chat with. To start, you only need to initiate one conversation a week, and the conversation can be on any topic that comes most easily to you. Once you get comfortable with that goal, you can increase the goal to twice a week or more frequently until you are striking up conversations every day.

This simple practice of initiating conversations helped me tremendously, not just in my professional life but in my personal one too. When I first moved from Ohio to New York City, I was truly on my own; I didn't know a single person in the Big Apple. It would have been easy to resign myself to a lackluster social life until I slowly made work buddies and such, but I knew I wanted to quickly build friendships and networks. So, I put myself out there. Whenever I found myself in a situation where I could meet new people, I put on a smile, introduced myself, and made small talk. I did this even in those times I felt scared and way out of my comfort zone. I'm happy to report that my efforts did pay off! In just a few short months of living in the city, I was able to build a solid network of friends. This experience taught me that the good things in life truly exist outside our comfort zone.

So I encourage you to get out there too. Once starting conversations becomes second nature, you can set more challenging goals for yourself that require you to practice your negotiation skills. Whether it's politely asking a noisy neighbor to turn down their music or suggesting lunch to a coworker you haven't broken bread with before, making a small request can be a great step in beginning to assert your needs and wants. You can also engage in small-stakes negotiations, such as asking for a discount at the farmers market or requesting a lower rate for your magazine subscription. Negotiating in these situations will be helpful to you even if you don't get what you set out to negotiate for! Even if the farmer says prices are firm or subscription discounts aren't available, you'll have gotten more practice at negotiating, and you'll have learned that hearing no is not so scary after all.

Once the small asks get easier, you can slowly work your way up to tougher work-related negotiations, whether it's more flexible hours to allow you to more easily drop off or pick up your kids from school, personal time off to take care of out-of-work duties on your plate, or a promotion to a leadership position that you know you're qualified for.

4. Prepare

Some negotiations can be undertaken on the fly, but others do require more thought. For more high-stakes negotiations, you might find it helpful to rehearse what you're going to say before going into the discussion. Consider asking a friend, colleague, or helpful mentor to talk through or even re-enact the negotiation with you, then ask these supporters for constructive feedback so you can be well prepared.

Practicing negotiations out loud can be invaluable in getting you comfortable with the act of negotiating in general. By saying what you want aloud, you can hear your tone, get a sense of your body language, and troubleshoot accordingly. In some ways, negotiating can be like a performance and performances go a lot better if you rehearse beforehand. By practicing, you'll find that you'll become less likely to stumble over words which will also help build your confidence.

If you're not sure how to begin or follow through on a big negotiation discussion, consider following a script. Start by writing down the specific asks you want to make, the points you want to hit, and the potential counterarguments you may want to address. Then, create a negotiation script for yourself to order and arrange your ideas. Of course, you don't need to memorize and follow the script word for word. However, having a very clear sense of the general outline of the conversation you'd like to have can be very helpful in preparing you for key discussions.

5. Listen Up

Sometimes, in our attempt to become better negotiators, we can get so focused on what we want for ourselves that we forget to pay attention to the needs of others. Yet, when we don't listen to others, we lose a valuable opportunity to see the topic from others' points of view and to find creative solutions. After all, the person you're negotiating with might have a better idea than you do for creating a win-win situation!

Of course, you do need to speak up and state what you want in a negotiation. After making your ask in a clear and direct manner, redirect your energies and attention toward listening to what the other party or parties have to say. Even if they say things you don't initially want to hear—like how difficult it is for the company to give anyone a raise at this time—you'll get a clearer sense of the other concerns surrounding the issue and thus be in a better position to advocate for your side. By knowing what the other parties are thinking about, you can then reframe the negotiation as a discussion focused on meeting everyone's needs, not just your own.

You may not have an immediate suggestion or solution to the points that other parties in the negotiation bring up. In this case, give yourself and others a little time to think. Negotiations don't have to be filled with chatter the entire time. Make room for silences here and there so that people have an opportunity to think through what has been said and come up with new solutions. You can even state directly that you need a moment to think through something that has been said to buy yourself a little more time. Resist the urge to fill up quiet moments. Silences can be very powerful.

Remember, you must negotiate to get those things you want, whether in business or in life. If you don't ever make it to the negotiating table, to begin with, you can't get the things you seek because you never give yourself the chance to even ask for them. To become a better negotiator, you need to get comfortable asking for what you want and be comfortable with hearing no at times. Getting a no isn't a devastating result to be feared, as it generally leaves you in no worse a position than you were in to begin with.

If the idea of negotiating still feels daunting to you, consider learning from someone who is already a pro at negotiating. Pay attention to how this person negotiates effectively during meetings and other office interactions, and if it's a possibility, ask if you can be a fly on the wall at their negotiation meetings. Seeing how an expert gets through negotiations will likely give you some clear ideas about how to better manage your own.

Remember, you can overcome your fear of negotiation step-by-step. Don't get discouraged if you don't transform into a fearless negotiator overnight. Negotiating is a learned skill, and as you practice it, you will get better. You'll learn to negotiate in a style that is a natural extension of your personality, being assertive without being aggressive, and acting as an excellent advocate for yourself without coming off as overly demanding.

7

BUILDING EFFECTIVE AND HIGH-PERFORMING TEAMS

> *"Leadership is about making others better as a result of your presence, and making sure that impact lasts in your absence."*

— SHERYL SANDBERG, COO OF FACEBOOK

Every leader works with and guides people, collaborating in teams to achieve larger successes together. This means that to be a great leader, you need to be great at building teams and to be a great team member yourself. You need to think about not just working well as an individual but also working well as part of a group.

Team building is not always an easy task. After all, every person is different, with different ideas, habits, and preferences. We all have opinions about how best to go about accomplishing a goal, what steps to take to streamline work, and which goals are worthy of pursuit. However, these opinions may not always align. Even when all team members are wonderful individuals, sometimes getting all these individuals to agree to work together toward a common goal in an efficient way can be challenging. The challenge for you, then, as a leader or leader in the making, is to learn how to build effective and high-performing teams.

STEPS TO BUILDING A HIGH-PERFORMING TEAM

To create a high-performing team, we must first understand exactly what a high-performing team is. The Society for Human Resources Management (SHRM) defines a high-performance team as "a group of goal-focused individuals with specialized expertise and complementary skills who collaborate, innovate and produce consistently superior results."[1]

Essentially, we're talking about a number of people working together to succeed at achieving a common goal. This means that the unique strengths of each individual on the team must be carefully considered. To create not merely a team but a high-performing team, you must choose team members who have the skill sets necessary to complete the goal at hand. A high-functioning marketing team, for example, shouldn't include only a bunch of social media managers. Rather, this kind of team should include a variety of people with different areas of expertise. A content marketer to write website copy and blog posts, a growth marketer to take charge of ads and sponsorship opportunities, and a product marketer to liaise closely with the sales team—these are all important roles that many marketing teams need to fill.

Once you know the skill sets you need to bring onto your team, you also need to make sure that the team members can function well together so that unnecessary conflicts don't arise, delaying you from reaching your goal. If there are known conflicts between certain employees at your company, you might look for ways to create groups that don't require people who already don't work well together to try to collaborate.

Every aspect of a high-functioning team, from the people you choose to the way you work together to the goal you set, is important to keep in mind. All of these aspects, in combination, are what make or break a team. While there are many ways to build a team, these are the six most important steps to keep in mind for high-functioning teams that you bring together:

1. Understand the goals for your team

Before you hire a team, you must have a very clear sense of what your end goals are for the team. Knowing this will help determine the type of team you create and the individuals you choose to join the team. If your ultimate goal is to develop a new software program, your team's size, structure, and makeup will be very different than if your goal is to improve customer service ratings, for example. For the former, you might hire mostly engineers with a leader or two to spearhead specific projects. For the latter, you may first need experts who can figure out what in the customer journey is responsible for lower-than-ideal ratings before you can even decide which additional members of the team to bring on. If the issue is a glitch in the order processing software, for example, you may need to hire engineers, but if the issue is long wait times to reach a customer support representative via phone, your best bet may be to hire additional representatives.

As you can see, it's important to understand what the needs for your project or goal are before adding people to your team. Once you have a concrete vision of your goal, you'll be in a much better position to determine how many team members you need, what skills they need to have, and whom to assign to which tasks.

2. Inspire your team

Simply assigning tasks to individual team members isn't the end all and be all of being a great leader. After all, people work best when they feel they have a connection and purpose regarding the goal at hand. For this reason, it's essential to pay close attention to motivating your team members at an emotional level. High-performing team leaders know just how important it is to cultivate an energy that catalyzes individuals to work toward a common goal.

How you inspire your team will depend strongly on the type of team you have. While some teams, like those in design or construction, tend to work very closely together, others, like those in engineering, tend to have their members work independently most of the time, coming together only for brief meetings and updates. Keep the overall structure of the team and the personalities of the individuals in mind when determining the best methods for inspiring your team.

Start by ensuring that your team members feel an individual connection to the goal at hand. This requires you as the leader to consider not just the overall goal for your team but also smaller, more personal goals for each member of the team. Consider how every single member can grow through participating in this team.

What will make them feel challenged to do their best? What will engage them intellectually and emotionally? To find answers to these questions, you might find it helpful to set up one-on-one meetings with each individual on your team, during which you can discuss personal work, career, skill, and performance goals to work toward. A team goal to add a new software service for the company could also be an opportunity for an individual coder to show how well they can create new software from scratch or a project manager to illustrate their ability to keep complex goals on track.

Once you've connected with the individual members of your team, think about how you can get those members to collaborate most effectively. Optimizing the efficiency of your team is crucial for ensuring that the group remains high performing. If appropriate, you might consider investing in collaboration tools or software, especially if your team members work remotely.

I also recommend regularly auditing team processes. How is a task handed off from one person to the next? Is this handoff process smooth and efficient? What could be done to make the workflow more seamless? How often are team meetings held, and how long do they typically last? Are there repetitive or unnecessary time-wasting actions that could be eliminated? Keep an eye out for creative ways to improve your team's efficiency so that all members can take care of their duties more efficiently.

3. Set goals

A team can be cooperative, motivated, and efficient, but without a clear common goal, the team won't achieve much. As the leader, it's your responsibility to clarify for the team what exactly you plan to achieve together. This includes setting the overarching vision and primary goals for the team, as well as setting individual goals for the various members of your team. Take a bird's-eye view approach to consider how the pieces of a project or plan fit together, so you can ensure that each person is given the right duties, roles, and responsibilities.

Put goals in place either before or very soon after you create your team. From the get-go, each person involved should have a sense of how they fit into the overall plan. A marketing person writing the ad copy for a new product will likely feel more motivated by knowing how this new product will help the people who buy it, for example.

Engaging the members of your team with the larger goal is also important to ensure that the milestones and deadlines you set as the leader are realistic. When everyone knows what is to be done and how it is to be accomplished, it's easier for all to predict when more resources may be needed or if it is essential to add another person to the team. In addition, individual members will have an idea of where various aspects of the project are so they can best determine when to step in to perform their duties. This will help with efficient team time management.

Make sure that each team member has a very clear sense of what their role is in the team and what individual duties they are responsible for. This way, you can prevent team members from unintentionally duplicating each other's efforts or leaving an important aspect of a project undone due to assumptions that someone else was responsible for it. It can be tiring and demoralizing for team members to discover that they've done unnecessary work due to suboptimal communication. So put processes in place to ensure that there is no confusion about who is in charge of what. Clearly defining people's roles also helps streamline working relationships in general. With defined roles, team members are also able to easily figure out exactly whom to go to with questions or requests for updates.

Of course, team goals, and individual goals, too, for that matter, don't have to be completely set-in stone. As your team works toward goals, you may find that your initial plans need to be tweaked, substantially revised, replaced, or scrapped altogether. Give yourself and your team enough flexibility that you can take advantage of new opportunities as they arise, or course correct for unexpected obstacles or challenges. Doing so will help you reach your goals efficiently, sometimes even more quickly and easily than you believed at the outset!

You might also consider setting not just one monolithic goal but instead putting in place several goal posts, ranging from very specific short-term goals to more fluid longer-term goals. Coming up with stretch goals —aiming at higher successes in case you reach your initial goal more quickly or easily than anticipated— can also be a motivating way to push and engage your team. You might, for example, have a goal for your sales team to bring on 100 new clients but also set a stretch goal to bring on 120, perhaps with an additional incentive for the team members to push for this tougher goal. This way, should you reach the initial goal quickly, you have a secondary goal to aim for and be excited about.

Once you set your goals, you need to also figure out how you're going to ensure that you meet those goals. Put processes in place to make sure that projects are progressing according to plan or that you're informed as quickly as possible if changes to the plan are necessary. Accountability measures are necessary not only for keeping goals on track but also for communication within the team. Give your team members an opportunity to inform others about the progress they're making on their individual duties at predetermined intervals. Whether formal or informal, these planned updates can serve as effective accountability measures for the team as a whole.

4. Communicate

You've heard the saying: A stitch in time saves nine. This adage holds true in the business world for projects and goals in progress, too. It's a lot easier to fix small issues and concerns as they arise than to troubleshoot after problems have already grown unwieldy. Looking into adding a customer service representative when customer hold times have increased by a minute or two is a lot easier than trying to deal with hold times after they've increased by an hour and made for very angry customers, to boot. Thus, leaders need to ensure that they learn about challenges, roadblocks, delays, or even potential delays as soon as possible so that the team can begin managing them right away.

How can you make sure you're always in the know? Open up the communication lines. As a leader, you are responsible for keeping your team members informed. Since high-performing teams often have members with very different skills in different areas, not all of them are going to know what the others are up to, and not all may understand the ease or difficulty of the task's others are taking on. Consider what level and frequency of communication are necessary to ensure the people you work with are up to date. Let them know about any changes or updates, so everyone is on the same page. You can achieve this through a mix of regular meetings and day-to-day communication tools that let team members share information in a way that is easy for all to access and refer back to as necessary.

Make sure that communication travels in all directions. News shouldn't always go just from you to the people you manage. Make it clear to your team members that they can come to you to discuss issues they may encounter, whether it's ideas for achieving goals more efficiently, troubleshooting concerns for particular projects, personality conflicts that may be happening between members of the team, or anything else. Keeping communication lines open will also help build trust—both trust in you from the people you manage, and the trust team members have for each other.

5. Build trust

It's not easy to follow in the footsteps of a person you don't have much confidence in. That's why, as a leader, it's crucial to be trusted by your team. From inspiring the team to move toward a common goal to navigating complexities that inevitably arise in business, your team members depend on you. You, too, need to be able to depend on your team members to accomplish their individual goals and pull their weight. For your team to reach high performance goals, trust between all members of your team is essential.

To build trust, you need to strike the right balance between supporting your team members toward reaching their goals and giving them room to forge their own paths to success. Resist the urge to micromanage processes or get too involved in the minutia of any one person's duties. After all, a big part of managing a high-performance team is allowing each of the members of the team to do what they do best. Allow the people you manage to work independently and exercise their expertise and skills. Give your team members opportunities to make decisions without consulting you every step of the way. When people are given the opportunity to work autonomously within the broader guidelines of the overall project and in light of the company mission and goals, of course, they are more likely to perform at a high level.

Building trust also requires giving all members of the team a stake in the collective goal. This includes creating opportunities for the people you manage to contribute to the overall decision-making process for the team. In the vast majority of cases, it's a bad idea to simply decide on a course of action on your own and then tell people what to do. Ask individuals what courses of action they recommend, what potential challenges to watch out for, and how best they think collective goals can be achieved.

6. Resolve conflict

Teamwork is what makes a team. Thus, as a leader, you must make sure not only that individuals are given autonomy to do their unique jobs but also that collaboration happens smoothly, as a matter of course, with as little friction as possible. You want your team members to work in a united fashion, trusting each other's abilities and relying on each other to get the necessary tasks done.

Your role as the leader includes minimizing conflicts as much as possible and easing conflicts that come up as quickly and positively as possible. As we discussed earlier in this chapter, allowing for open communication to reduce misunderstandings is a highly effective way to prevent many conflicts before they even arise. Lack of communication is a real productivity killer because of the potential it creates for conflicts. Prioritize keeping everyone apprised of essential information, and your team will free itself from time-sucking conflicts that stymie many less productive teams.

When team conflicts arise, and trust me, they will, I recommend addressing them directly and early on. Ignoring conflicts will rarely make them go away; it's much more likely that these conflicts will fester and keep growing, creating rifts in the team and disruptions in the workflow. Don't let small disagreements turn into gigantic problems. Dealing with conflict is often an uncomfortable experience, but this discomfort is something all leaders need to tackle head-on.

What steps can you take to quickly diffuse and resolve problems that come up within a team? One key thing to try is reminding the members of your team that we are, in fact, all on the same team. Since we are working toward the same goal, we don't need to compete with each other. We can get where we're all going a lot faster if we choose to cooperate instead.

Teams are common to every business, but not every business can boast of having high-performing teams. In your career, you've probably seen teams that bicker internally, don't collaborate, and sometimes even sabotage each other's work. Your goal is to nurture a team that truly works together. Such teams require great leadership, and following the tips in this chapter will better prepare you to be the kind of inspiring leader that catalyzes high-performing teams.

8

STORIES FROM SUCCESSFUL WOMEN

S tepping into a leadership role can feel daunting. I myself have experienced fear, self-doubt, and even stage fright while guiding the teams I've managed or serving as the keynote speaker at large events. Yet, I've learned and grown every time I've faced those challenging emotions and led through them. I, and many other women leaders today, know through experience that great leadership skills can be practiced, internalized, and taught to others.

Seeing other women step up and succeed in leadership roles has been a great inspiration to me in my career in business, so I wanted to share some stories of inspirational female leaders with you too. As you'll see, all of these amazing leaders encountered significant hurdles in their careers. They faced up to both expected and unexpected challenges, fastballs and curveballs, straight shots, and circuitous paths to success. I hope reading these women's stories encourages you to take on challenges of your own so you, too, can soon be an inspirational story to other would-be female leaders.

Sara Blakely – Founder and CEO of Spanx

Whether you love them or hate them, I'm sure you've heard of Spanx shapewear. What you may not have heard is the story of how Spanx first came about as a business idea. This is not the typical story of a startup, where a few savvy business school graduates come together in an incubator and get millions of dollars in funding from venture fund companies for their great new idea. No, Spanx's success took a much more individualistic path and, in fact, comes from a string of what many would have seen as career failures.

While Sara Blakely may be famous as the creator of Spanx today, she did not always dream of being a shapewear mogul. As a young woman, she wanted a completely different career as an attorney. Her father was a lawyer and a shining example for her. So Sara was determined to follow in his footsteps. Becoming a lawyer requires going to law school, however. Unfortunately for Blakely, her LSAT scores—she took the law school admission test twice—were quite low.

So instead of starting law school, Blakely ended up taking a string of seemingly random jobs, ranging from working a ride at Disney World to selling fax machines for an office supply company. These jobs weren't exactly glamorous, but they did help Blakely discover some important insights about herself. She learned, for example, that although she wasn't great at scoring high on the LSAT, she was quite good at selling things—even fax machines.

Her jobs, which required Blakely to wear pantyhose, also helped her spot an opportunity to create a new clothing niche. The shaping and molding qualities of pantyhose smoothed the way Blakely's body looked underneath her clothes, and seeing this effect made Blakely realize other women also might be interested in wearing similar garments. That gave her the idea to create shapewear, and thus, Spanx was born.

Of course, launching Spanx as a business involved much more than simply coming up with an idea. According to a Forbes profile[1], Blakely did everything from researching and applying for patents to calling up pantyhose companies to pitch her product to stores. Blakely did all this while still working full time at the office supply company! It required a lot of time, effort, and determination.

Having limited funds available meant Blakely did all her own marketing and public relations legwork. She slowly got her brand out there and into big-name stores like Neiman Marcus. Soon, her products were getting a lot of attention from tastemakers like Oprah Winfrey. By 2012, she was named by TIME magazine as one of the 100 most influential people in the world. Today, Spanx is a household name and Blakely's brand encompasses an entire fashion line that includes dresses, activewear, and swimwear. The company continues to expand, more recently having moved into menswear and denim too. Last year, Blackstone took a majority stake in Spanx. Once that deal closes, Blakely will be able to change her role in the company to that of executive chairwoman. Blakely is also well known as a philanthropist; she launched the Spanx by Sara Blakely Foundation with the goal to support and empower women-owned businesses.

Blakely's story is an inspiring one because her career path was far from direct. It's the story of a woman who had to go through a big disappointment relatively early on in life, giving up her dream of becoming a lawyer, as well as a long transitional phase during a time when her jobs weren't exactly the fulfillment of her life's dream. Yet, Blakely didn't give up.

What I find especially touching about Blakely's story is that she decided to pursue her shapewear idea even while she had a comfortable job at the office supply company where she was working. I think many of us tend to take jobs that aren't our dream jobs, then stay there, sometimes for life, because we are comfortable enough, and we don't care to put in the time, effort, and energy to actually go after our bigger dreams. Yet, Blakely reached for something more. She had a spark of an idea, then followed it doggedly until she saw it through—not just creating a company but growing it at an exponential rate until it was valued at over a billion dollars. The valuation is impressive, of course, but what is most impressive is Blakely's grit and stick-to-itiveness.

Have you also had an earlier goal that you had to set aside? If so, don't despair. It's not at all uncommon to go down one path in life to discover that your true path is actually a different one. Like Blakely, you, too, can figure things out by trial and error until you figure out the leadership goal you're best suited for. Be patient! Your first, second, or even third job may not be the exact thing you may want to do, but they'll all likely teach you lessons that foster your future success. Keep pursuing your goals until you do succeed, without letting low test scores, bad jobs, or failed opportunities stop you from pushing forward. Have faith in your ideas and yourself and think long term about your business and career trajectory.

Ursula Burns – Former CEO of Xerox

What does it take to break boundaries and glass ceilings? To get the answer to that question, there's no better place to look than the story of Ursula Burns. This woman grew up in the New York City projects with a single mother, then became the very first African-American woman CEO of a Fortune 500 company when she took the top position at Xerox back in 2009.

Burns didn't start out on top, though. In fact, her first position at Xerox was that of an intern! She started at the company full time after getting her bachelor's in mechanical engineering and her Master of Science in mechanical engineering from Columbia. From there, she went up and up and up, going from assistant to vice president of global manufacturing all the way to CEO.

Her tenure at Xerox was obviously a long one, during which she hung out and learned from company leaders and got a close look at the business from the bottom up. The team Burns led, in fact, came up with network printers, a technology widely used across the globe today.

Burns stepped down from her CEO role once Xerox split into two companies in 2016. After that, she served as the CEO of VEON, an international telecom company. Under the Obama administration, Burns became the leader of the White House National STEM program. Now, she also serves as a founding member of Change the Equation, a nonprofit dedicated to promoting STEM education.

Burns's story is an inspiring one today, a time when many people change jobs every year or two, bouncing through companies in search of slightly higher pay or benefits. I find it pretty amazing that she truly went from intern to CEO, even though the process obviously took some years. Becoming a leader doesn't require complicated job-hopping strategies through a series of companies. Burns shows us that we can indeed rise up the ranks to take the top position at a place that rewards us for our contribution, loyalty, and continued push for innovation.

Perhaps, just like Burns, you are already at a company you like and want to grow with. If so, take Burns as your model. Focus on how you can take on leadership roles within your company, looking at internal opportunities that let you develop new skills and take on more managerial duties. If your goal is to eventually become the CEO, plan out some potential paths to get you from the position you hold now to that top role. Having a clear path in mind can help focus your energies and motivate you to engage more fully with your company, taking on increasingly bigger and more indispensable roles as your tenure increases. Learn from the leaders who currently hold the positions you'd like to hold one day and don't forget to take the time to nurture and mentor the women leaders coming up after you. They'll look up to you as the example to follow so they also can take leadership roles in the future.

Rea Ann Silva – Founder and CEO of Beautyblender

You don't have to have a business school background to become a successful businesswoman. In fact, you can just start with what you already know, even if it doesn't seem like a business idea on its own and build your unique brand from there. That's a fact that becomes very clear when looking at Rea Ann Silva's career trajectory.

If you wear makeup, chances are you're familiar with Rea Ann Silva's makeup applicator, better known as the Beautyblender. This tool is a staple of women's makeup bags and certainly of makeup professionals' kits today. Yet, there was a time when this popular, near-ubiquitous item didn't exist! Back when Rea Ann Silva was working as a makeup artist, she actually had to fashion her own sponges because the ones that came from the store just didn't do what she wanted them to do. To create the flawless complexion she wanted for the actors whose makeup she did, she made her own makeup sponge at home, cutting up triangle wedges to make them more rounded. The rounded sponge allowed for improved makeup looks. Soon, Silva realized that others would see the beauty of her beauty tool, too, if she made it available for sale.

Thus, the Beautyblender was created in 2003. Slowly, independent professional beauty stores started picking it up, and word of mouth spread. More and more makeup lovers started seeking out the Beautyblender. Sometime later, Sephora picked up the product, taking it nationwide. As Silva's story shows, inspiration can come from the work you're already doing. Silva found a way to do her job as a makeup artist more easily and efficiently, then turned that idea into a profitable business.

What ideas do you have that could be valuable? You don't have to look far from your day-to-day routine to get the answer to this question. Rather, consider what you are doing right now in your current role. Do you see ways you could find the tasks you're doing more easily, smoothly, or efficiently? Are there tools or hacks you've jerry-rigged together that you think others would want to know about? Do colleagues come to you for advice and ideas on how to make projects go better? If so, this is knowledge that you and others can use. Don't discount the small improvements you've made to improve your work. Whether you have created new shortcuts, tools, or products, are able to offer mentorship or education, or know a new method of getting things done at your current place of work, the information you have is valuable.

Mary Barra – CEO of General Motors

Mary Barra is another woman who has made big business history. Back in 2014, she became the first female CEO of an auto manufacturer when she took the top spot at General Motors. By 2017, she was the highest paid executive among Big Three U.S. automobile manufacturers.

General Motors is, of course, a huge company involved with everything from the design and manufacturing of vehicles to distribution, sales, and maintenance. The company has many divisions and subdivisions, with offices around the country and the world. However, Barra is one person who really knew the company well, having learned about it from the ground up. By the time she made it to the CEO position, Barra had been a very long-time employee of General Motors. She started working for the company when she was still a student, checking fenders. She went to work for General Motors full time once she graduated from college, moving up through a wide number of positions in management, administration, and engineering over her decades-long tenure. The titles she held at General Motors are quite varied, in fact. In vice president roles alone, she headed up global manufacturing engineering, global human resources, and global product at different points in her career. She really got to know the company from many different angles.

Once she became CEO, Barra had to take on some huge challenges for the company, including a number of safety recalls that she had to testify about in the Senate. But Barra led the company through these difficult times, with General Motors instituting new policies to help prevent such safety issues in the future. Barra also oversaw the company as it started developing electric vehicles, including the Chevy Volt EV, which came to the market in 2017. Today, she is overseeing the company's continued push into the electric vehicle market.

Barra's story is really an inspiring one for women who want to make history. She entered an industry dominated by men and climbed through the ranks while exploring so many different aspects of business. Though she stayed at one company, her career was wide-ranging; she gained skills and experience in a variety of departments. I'm awed by Barra's willingness to push herself to become an expert in many different fields—knowledge that I'm sure serves her well as she continues to oversee GM today. If you also are a woman who likes to break boundaries and take on big challenges, Barra serves as an excellent example of how far you can go and what heights you can reach.

Indra Nooyi – Former CEO of PepsiCo

PepsiCo is a gigantic company with brands recognized around the world, including Pepsi, of course, but also other well-known names such as Tropicana, Quaker Oats, and Gatorade. For a number of years, a woman, Indra Nooyi, led this global conglomerate as the chairperson and CEO. Nooyi's contribution to the business world was a groundbreaking one. When she took on this role in 2006, she became the first woman of color and immigrant to lead a Fortune 500 company.

How did Nooyi come to make her mark in the business world? This leader's life and career path took her across both industries and continents. Nooyi was born and grew up in India before moving to the United States to study at the Yale School of Management, eventually earning a master's in public and private management. For a while, she worked for other organizations, then began consulting for

PepsiCo, but then joined the company full time in 1994, climbing up the ranks until she was named CEO.

At PepsiCo, Nooyi was known for redirecting the company through an effort called Performance with a Purpose. Through this initiative, Nooyi pushed the company toward healthier foods and more sustainable practices through recycling initiatives, packaging redesign, and the use of renewable energy. She led the company until 2018, when she stepped from the CEO role, then also stepped down from her chairperson role in 2019.

Nooyi has garnered many honors, both within and beyond the world of business. Not only has she been inducted into the Asian Hall of Fame, but she was also named the first international female director of the International Cricket Council. Clearly, despite what must be a very busy work schedule, this business execu-tive still made time to nurture hobbies that were important to her!

Nooyi's story especially inspires me because she combined her passion for making the world a better place with her passion for business. Nooyi didn't have to push PepsiCo to get healthier and greener, but she chose to, even when she faced opposition and obstacles. As a result, she's given us healthier foods and a cleaner

148 | LINDSEY BEGUE

environment. At the same time, she helped shape a more positive image for the brand she represented.

Do you also have health, environmental, or social justice goals you'd like to pursue? If so, I think Nooyi's life and career trajectory gives you a lot to learn from. Making a positive difference in the world doesn't require you to work for nonprofits or foundations. However, you can certainly choose to go that route if you'd like to. Nooyi shows that whatever organization you work for, big or small, you can push it to become better—not just at making money or succeeding in business but also at making the world a better place for all.

Susan Wojcicki – CEO of YouTube

Susan Wojcicki is an inspiration for women in technology. Named the CEO of YouTube in 2014, Wojcicki has become one of the most prominent names in business today and a well-recognized figure in tech circles. In 2015, she made it to TIME's list of 100 most influential people, which really comes as no surprise, as YouTube is a highly successful and popular company whose platform is used by millions of people and companies each day.

Wojcicki didn't start out at YouTube's top spot. Her career trajectory first took her through several other companies until she joined Google as one of the original employees, taking on a marketing manager role in 1999. By 2003, she had moved on to a product management role, overseeing the then-new advertising product called AdSense. She rose up the ranks and spearheaded more and more of Google's business, including Google's video service. That's when Wojcicki spearheaded the decision to buy a startup company called YouTube, the purchase of which she managed.

With Wojcicki heading up YouTube, the video streaming service grew exponentially. Today, YouTube is available in more than a hundred countries around the world. People use it for so many different purposes, ranging from learning yoga to watching music videos to picking up a new language. YouTube also serves as a platform that allows for many content creators to earn a living through their work by directly reaching their audiences.

For me, Wojcicki's story is a reminder that we can truly learn what we need to learn on the job. After all, Wojcicki didn't have any big corporate executive experience when she joined Google. Rather, she started out in what many would call a more niche role in marketing, an area in which she already had some experience from previous jobs. Wojcicki also chose not to take the traditional career path of a marketer, moving linearly from manager to director to vice president in that field. Instead, she branched out to product management, creatively producing new streams of income for Google. She also kept an eye on the competition, learning about YouTube and making the decision to snap it up before taking charge of it and growing it to the influential platform it is today. She also took on the challenge of running YouTube, taking it through a huge transformation in technologies around the world.

If you're a big thinker who likes to find new, creative solutions, you'll likely find Wojcicki's career inspiring. She shows that you can succeed by taking a chance with a small startup, then growing with it until it becomes a world-changing force. She also shows that you can start in pretty much any field, whether it's marketing, product development, or sales.

The old stereotypes still exist today. Ask someone to picture a CEO, and the vision will likely be that of a man in a suit. Many women still find themselves the only female member of a board, the only female leader at a meeting, and the only female entrepreneur at a business networking event. Yet, as you can see from the examples above, many women are breaking those stereotypes, setting new standards, and stepping into new roles that women haven't taken on before.

That's not to say it's easy to become a female leader in business. Women CEOs today still tend to be the exception rather than the rule. There are still many cultural biases that work against women. The results of those biases can be seen in the numbers. For example, women-led startups still have a lot more difficulties than those led by men when it comes to getting investments both from individuals and venture capital firms.

Yet, it is worth it to step up and go for those leadership roles, even if you might at times feel that the deck is stacked against you. After all, there are good reasons why you want to become a leader, right? Keep that vision of yourself strong by keeping in mind the inspiring stories of the female leaders that have come before you. These women had goals of their own and pursued them until they made them a reality. Knowing what kind of difference you want to make as a leader can be helpful too. Do you want to make life for women more convenient, comfortable, or beautiful through new products in the vein of Spanx or the Beauty-blender? Or do you want to transform a company's status quo into one that is better for people and the planet, as Nooyi did for PepsiCo? Keeping this end goal in mind will help motivate you even when you face challenges along your path toward leadership.

After all, new opportunities are opening up in the world every day. The world of business is changing rapidly. Even in the last couple of years, we've seen dramatic alterations in the way people do their work. Before the coronavirus crisis, most people commuted to work every day as a matter of course. Today, a large percentage of employees work from home either some or part of the time. Businesses that offered services to make remote or distributed work easier and more productive suddenly saw a huge influx of interest and investment. We can't predict exactly how the world will change, but we can be open to adapting and stepping up as opportunities arise. By going after leadership roles, you may end up inventing a whole new category of consumer goods or a brand-new technology that transforms people's lives. Seize these opportunities even when success isn't certain, and the road looks long, hard, and arduous. You must say yes to the chances coming your way in order to attain your dreams. It's the only way to truly discover what you're capable of. Even when the traditional business world doesn't seem interested in what you have to offer, you must take yourself and your skills and experiences seriously. Do the research and work necessary to build your confidence, then trust that you have value to add.

Nothing worth having in life comes easily. Don't let longer timelines or unforeseen difficulties derail your efforts to step into leadership roles. The women whose stories we read took decades to get to the top positions they ended up taking on. As they made their way up, they gained a wide breadth of experience, picked up skills in numerous different areas of business, and learned from the other leaders around them. Make sure you allow yourself the opportunity to do the same in your leadership journey.

CONCLUSION

Leadership takes initiative. Even your favorite mentor or boss is unlikely to suddenly start showering you with opportunities you haven't asked for. This means you must make the ask and make a good case for the things you ask for. You need to look for opportunities, then go after them with gusto.

Throughout this book, you picked up tips and time-tested strategies for reaching your leadership goals. You read the stories of real female leaders who've come before you, whose examples you can look up to when crafting your own strategy for climbing the corporate ladder. You've received information on how to over-come your fears, what to do to be recognized for your talents, and why it's important to negotiate for the things you want. In the end, though, what you need most to become a leader is the desire and drive to lead.

It's this desire that will carry you forward, even when times get tough. After all, it's easy to keep moving forward when things already seem to be going your way. Getting a raise, promotion, or bonus tends to motivate people, prompting them to do what it takes to get to the next level. However, the path to leadership isn't going to be lined with successes all the time. There will come times when you don't get that promotion you thought was coming to you, when your request for a raise is denied summarily, and when your contribution to your company feels unvalued. You may face bitter disappointments too. Failures are, after all, frequent in both business and life. Downsizings, layoffs, company splits, and mergers—all of these are common in the business world today, and they can end up affecting your career plans in ways you did not expect.

It is in these challenging moments that you need to hold on tightly to your goal of becoming a leader. Don't give up! You need to remember in darker times not only your own personal career goals and dreams but also the example you're setting for the women who come after you. By striving for your own leadership goals, you show other women that they, too, can persevere and set a high bar for themselves and eventually succeed. By not giving up, you show other women that determination and action lead to long-term success.

Having read this book, you know that becoming a leader requires patience and fortitude. You've seen many examples of successful women who once were at the very bottom of the corporate ladder, working as interns or entry-level salespeople. These women plugged away at reaching their dreams for not just days, months, and years, but decades. As groundbreaking leaders, many of these women had very few examples of other female leaders to look up to for guidance. You, on the other hand, have a growing number of female entrepreneurs, bosses, and CEOs to emulate and learn from. You also have the knowledge you've gained from this book. You can use the information you learned to tackle whatever issues you may be facing in your career now.

The challenges women leaders face are many. There are cultural and societal issues that we still come up against, as well as our own emotional struggles and doubts. You may be working at a company where all the leaders are men and worry that none of them are ready to include a woman in their midst. You might pride yourself in your empathetic nature but recognize that the current leaders in your organization don't yet see the benefit of this relational quality. In short, you can certainly come up with many reasons not to try to become a leader, to decide it's too hard, and give up this goal before even starting on it. Yet, if we let these types of barriers block us, we can remain stuck forever.

I want you to use this book to get unstuck. Whether you feel you're often overlooked for promotions or worry that you still let imposter syndrome get the best of you, you now have the tools to change that and move on and up. If you're early on in your career, I hope this book gives you the courage and know-how to set a goal to land your first leadership role. If you're already in a leadership position, I hope this book has armed you with new tools to become an even better leader and move up even further in the organization. I want to see you as a reader of this book to one day step into your dream leadership role. I want you to be top entrepreneurs, CEOs, and board advisors.

So don't stop after reading this conclusion, closing the book and putting it away on a shelf to gather dust. Instead, go back to the beginning and start applying its lessons. The knowledge you've gained won't do much good unless you start using and applying them! Use your own empowerment to achieve that next promotion. Your path will likely be a lot smoother and faster than mine since you've already gained the tried-and-true lessons of leadership to speed you along.

Of course, don't stop at just reaching your own leadership goals. Help other women step into success also by supporting them, mentoring them, and sharing this book with them. The knowledge in this book will be invaluable for the women who come after you too, so pay it forward by putting the book in their hands. If you've found words of inspiration, guidance, and encouragement in this book, please consider leaving an honest review on Amazon, Goodreads, or other websites that will help women find their way to this guide. Reviews really do make a difference, and your recommendation could encourage another woman like you to step into greatness too.

Most importantly, get out there and start leading!

A FREE GIFT TO OUR READERS

Scan the QR code below to find out your leadership style

Or visit this link: http://bit.ly/3E7SJIA

NOTES

1. WHY FEMALE LEADERSHIP IS IMPORTANT

1. National Student Clearinghouse Research Center. (2022). *Overview: Spring 2022 enrollment estimates.* https://nscresearchcenter. org/wp-content/uploads/CTEE_Report_Spring_2022.pdf.
2. National Association of Law Placement. (2020). *Class of 2019 national summary report.* https://www.nalp.org/classof2019.
3. Association of American Medical Colleges. (2019, Dec. 9) *The majority of U.S. medical students are women, new data show.* https://www.aamc.org/news-insights/press-releases/majority-us-medical-students-are-women-new-data-show.
4. Hinchliffe, Emma. (2022, May 23). The number of women running Fortune 500 companies reaches a record high. *Fortune.* https://fortune.com/2022/05/23/female-ceos-fortune-500-2022-women-record-high-karen-lynch-sarah-nash/.
5. Rockefeller Foundation. (2016). *Women in leadership: Why it matters.* https://www.rockefellerfoundation.org/wp-content/uploads/Women-in-Leadership-Why-It-Matters.pdf.
6. United States Census Bureau. 2021. America's Families and Living Arrangements: 2021. Table FG6. One-parent Unmarried Family Groups with Own Children Under 18, by Marital Status of the Reference Person: 2021. https://www.census.gov/data/tables/2021/demo/families/cps-2021.html.

3. BUILDING CONFIDENCE AND DESTROYING IMPOSTER SYNDROME

1. Zenger, J. & J. Folkman. (2019, June) Research: Women score higher than men in most leadership skills. *Harvard Business Review*. https://hbr.org/2019/06/research-women-score-higher-than-men-in-most-leadership-skills.

7. BUILDING EFFECTIVE AND HIGH-PERFORMING TEAMS

1. Society of Human Resources Management. (2022). Developing and sustaining high performance work teams. https://www.shrm.org/resourcesandtools/tools-and-samples/toolkits/pages/developingandsustaininghigh-performanceworkteams.aspx.

8. STORIES FROM SUCCESSFUL WOMEN

1. O'Connor, Clare. (14 March, 2012). "How Sara Blakely of Spanx turned $5,000 into $1 billion." *Forbes*. https://www.forbes.com/global/2012/0326/billionaires-12-feature-united-states-spanx-sara-blakely-american-booty.html

REFERENCES

Association of American Medical Colleges. (2019, Dec. 9) *The majority of U.S. medical students are women, new data show.* https:// www.aamc.org/news-insights/press-releases/majority-us-medical-students-are-women-new-data-show

Hinchliffe, Emma. (2022, May 23). The number of women running Fortune 500 companies reaches a record high. *Fortune.* https:// fortune.com/2022/05/23/female-ceos-fortune-500-2022-women-record-high-karen-lynch-sarah-nash/

National Association of Law Placement. (2020). *Class of 2019 national summary report.* https://www.nalp.org/classof2019.

National Student Clearinghouse Research Center. (2022). *Over- view: Spring 2022 enrollment estimates.* https://nscresearchcenter.org/wp-content/uploads/CTEE_Report_Spring_2022.pdf

O'Connor, Clare. (14 March, 2012). "How Sara Blakely of   Spanx turned $5,000 into $1 billion." *Forbes.* https://www.forbes.com/global/2012/0326/billionaires-12-feature-united-states-spanx-sara-blakely-american-booty.html

Rockefeller Foundation. (2016). *Women in leadership: Why it matters.* https://www.rockefellerfoundation.org/wp-content/uploads/Women-in-Leadership-Why-It-Matters.pdf

Society of Human Resources Management. (2022). Developing and sustaining high performance work teams. https://www.shrm.org/resourcesandtools/tools-and-samples/toolkits/pages/developingandsustaininghigh-performanceworkteams.aspx

United States Census Bureau. 2021. America's Families and Living Arrangements: 2021. Table FG6. One-parent Unmarried Family Groups with Own Children Under 18, by Marital Status of the Reference   Person: 2021.   https://www.census.gov/data/tables/2021/demo/families/cps-2021.html

Zenger, J. & J. Folkman. (2019, June) Research: Women score higher than men in most leadership skills. *Harvard Business Review*. https:// hbr.org/2019/06/research-women-score-higher-than-men-in-most-leadership-skills

Printed in Great Britain
by Amazon